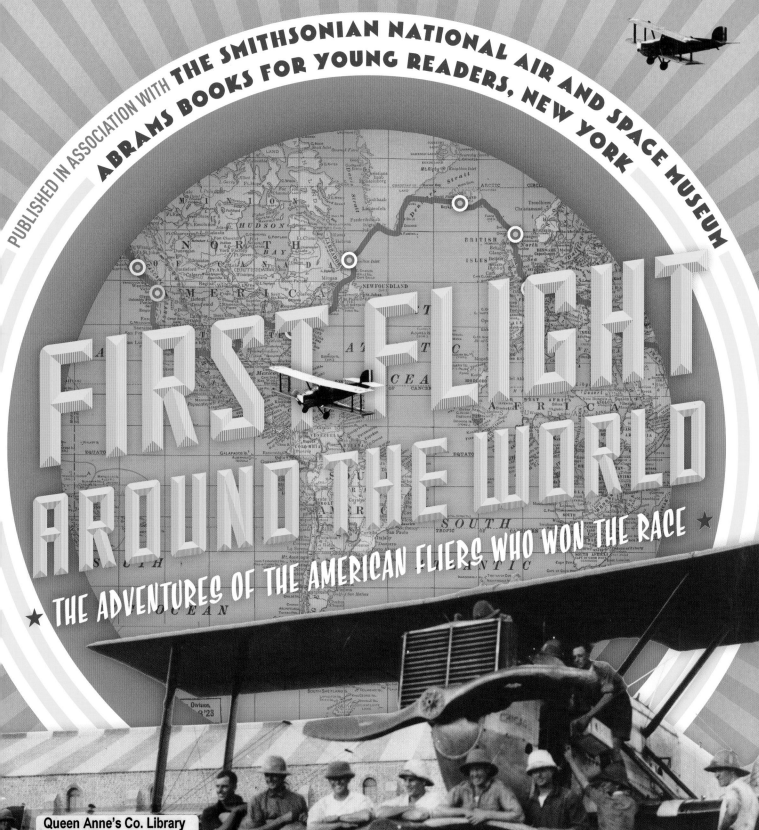

PUBLISHED IN ASSOCIATION WITH **THE SMITHSONIAN NATIONAL AIR AND SPACE MUSEUM**

ABRAMS BOOKS FOR YOUNG READERS, NEW YORK

FIRST FLIGHT AROUND THE WORLD

★ THE ADVENTURES OF THE AMERICAN FLIERS WHO WON THE RACE ★

BY TIM GROVE

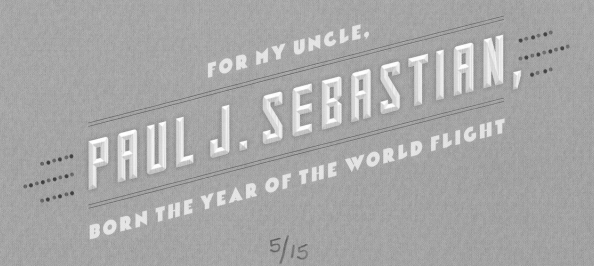

FOR MY UNCLE,
PAUL J. SEBASTIAN,
BORN THE YEAR OF THE WORLD FLIGHT

5/15

Library of Congress Cataloging-in-Publication Data

Grove, Tim, 1967–
First flight around the world : the adventures of the
American fliers who won the race / by Tim Grove.
pages cm.
Includes bibliographical references.
ISBN 978-1-4197-1482-5
1. Flights around the world—Juvenile literature. 2. United States. Army. Air Corps—Juvenile
literature. 3. World records—Juvenile literature. I. National Air and Space Museum. II. Title.
TL721.U6G58 2015
910.4'1—dc23
2014024665

Text copyright © 2015 The Smithsonian National Air and Space Museum
For illustration credits, see page 86.
Book design by Sara Corbett

Printed and bound in Singapore

10 9 8 7 6 5 4 3 2 1

Abrams Books for Young Readers are available at special
discounts when purchased in quantity for premiums and promotions
as well as fundraising or educational use. Special editions
can also be created to specification. For details, contact
specialsales@abramsbooks.com or the address below.

ABRAMS
THE ART OF BOOKS SINCE 1949

115 West 18th Street
New York, NY 10011
www.abramsbooks.com

CONTENTS

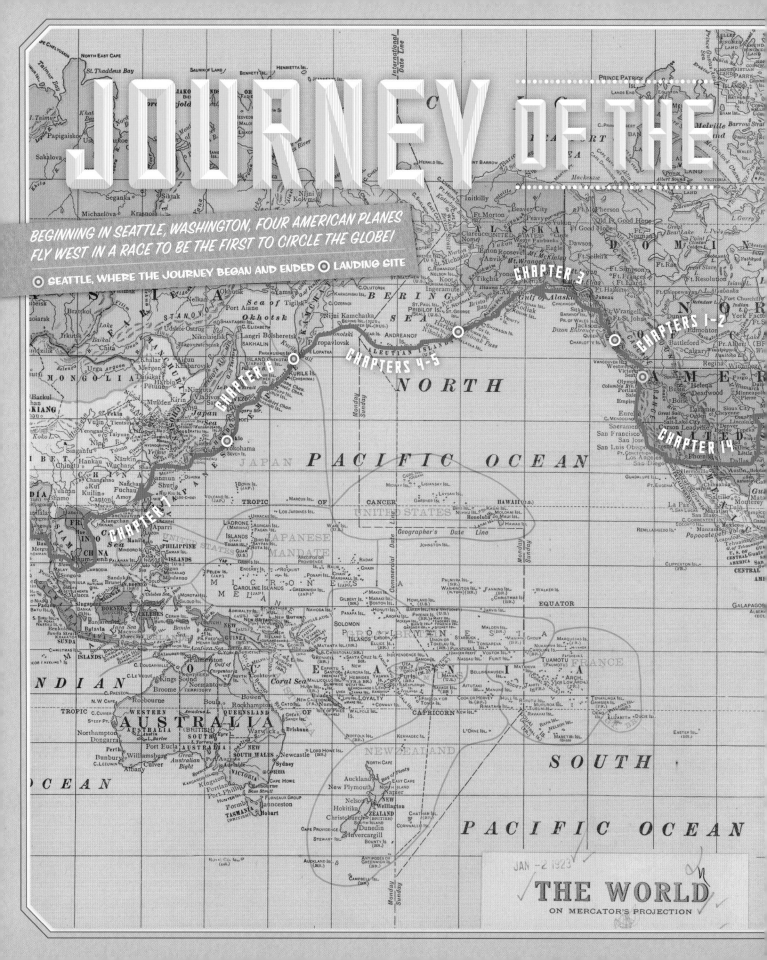

JOURNEY OF THE

BEGINNING IN SEATTLE, WASHINGTON, FOUR AMERICAN PLANES FLY WEST IN A RACE TO BE THE FIRST TO CIRCLE THE GLOBE!

◎ SEATTLE, WHERE THE JOURNEY BEGAN AND ENDED ◎ LANDING SITE

CHAPTER 3

CHAPTERS 1-2

CHAPTERS 4-5

CHAPTER 6

CHAPTER 14

CHAPTER 7

JAN -2 1923

THE WORLD
ON MERCATOR'S PROJECTION

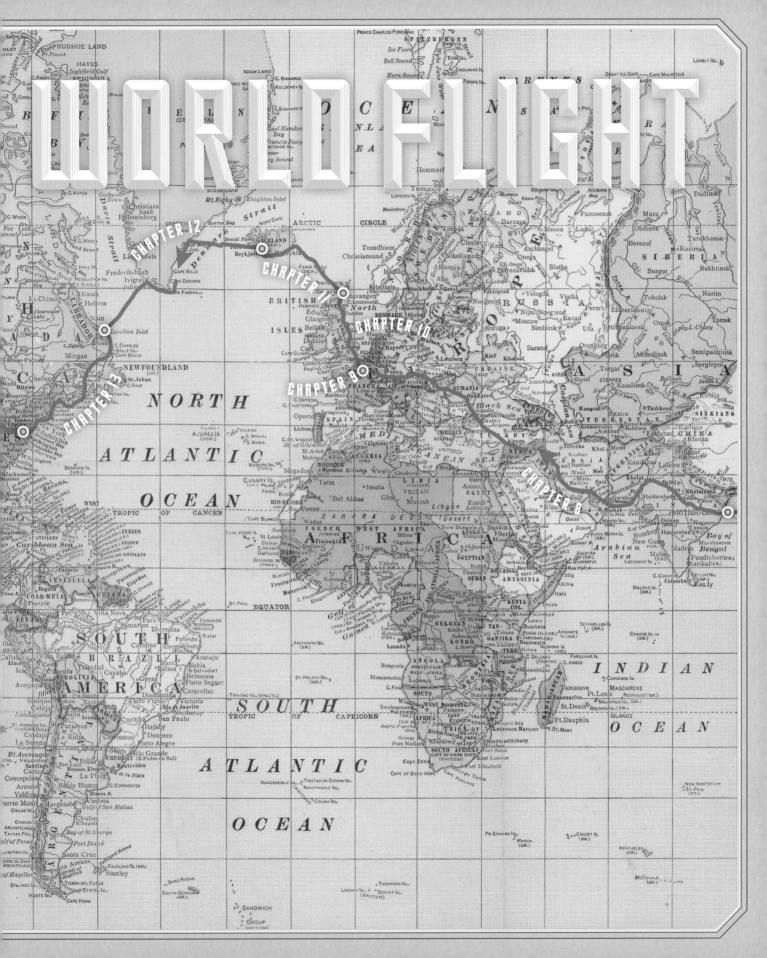

INTRODUCTION

When this story took place, the world was very different from what it is today. In the early 1920s, Europe was recovering from World War I, which had brought devastation and great hardship across the continent. Large parts of Asia and the Middle East that now are independent nations were governed by countries like Great Britain and France. To find out what was going on around the world, people read newspapers or watched newsreels—short film clips that were shown before the full-length movie at a theater. Radio, a recent invention, was increasing in popularity, but televisions, mobile phones, and the Internet did not exist. Women were just beginning to make gains in a male-dominated world and were in the process of earning the right to vote in many countries. Travel was very expensive, and people relied on trains or ocean liners to go long distances. Many people had never seen an airplane, except in pictures.

In 1924, the U.S. Army sent eight young men on a grand adventure around the world. It was not a voyage of exploration but rather a bold attempt to be the first to circumnavigate the globe by flight. Airmen from five other countries—Great Britain, France, Portugal, Italy, and Argentina—had the same goal, and so the quest became a race. Who would win?

The trip held many challenges: extreme weather, tricky navigation, fragile planes, a scarcity of airfields, and the necessity of dealing with unfamiliar countries and cultures. The world fliers would be risking their lives, facing one obstacle after another, for the sake of their country's pride. It would be an honor for the United States to be the first to conquer the world by air. For the fliers it was a once-in-a-lifetime opportunity.

THE OFFICIAL INSIGNIA THAT WAS PAINTED ON EACH PLANE. THE LIGHT BLUE CLOUD SHAPE FEATURED TWO BALD EAGLES, SYMBOLS OF THE UNITED STATES, CIRCLING A GLOBE.

Many men applied to go on the trip, but the Army needed only eight in all: four pilots and four mechanics. First Lieutenant Leslie Arnold was upset when he found out he had been selected as one of two alternate pilots; it appeared that he wouldn't be going. But then another person got sick and couldn't go, and so he joined the crew, although as a mechanic instead of a pilot. He would fly around the world in a plane named the *Chicago* and keep a journal of his experiences. Both the plane and the journal would one day end up in the Smithsonian National Air and Space Museum in Washington, D.C. More than 400 photographs taken on the flight would become part of the museum's archives. This account of the World Flight is based, in part, on Arnold's journal.

❶ THE NO. 1A AUTOGRAPHIC KODAK JR. CAMERA CARRIED BY LOWELL SMITH ON THE WORLD FLIGHT.

❷ THE FLIERS AT SAND POINT, WASHINGTON, AT THE BEGINNING OF THEIR FLIGHT [*FROM LEFT*]: ARTHUR TURNER (DID NOT GO ON FLIGHT), HENRY OGDEN, LESLIE ARNOLD, LEIGH WADE, LOWELL SMITH, FREDERICK MARTIN, ALVA HARVEY. ERIK NELSON AND JOHN HARDING ARE MISSING.

❸ THE *CHICAGO*, READY FOR TAKEOFF, WITH PILOT LOWELL SMITH AND MECHANIC LESLIE ARNOLD.

THE *BOSTON* TAKING OFF AT THE START OF THE FLIGHT.

THE JOURNEY BEGINS

APRIL 6, 1924

Around 8:30 A.M., on April 6, 1924, three airplanes floating on the calm water of Lake Washington in Seattle taxied away from their moorings, revved their engines, and climbed steadily into the cold, gray sky. A fourth plane, weighed down by supplies, could not break the surface tension of the water and returned to its mooring to unload some weight. After a delay, it managed to join the others aloft. The biplanes were named for four major American cities: *Seattle* (no. 1), *Chicago* (no. 2), *Boston* (no. 3), and *New Orleans* (no. 4). Each plane held a pilot

FLYING NEAR PRINCE RUPERT, BRITISH COLUMBIA.

and a mechanic, plenty of fuel (450 gallons), and various supplies. In addition, two small stuffed toy monkeys—good-luck charms—were along for the ride.

The eight airmen, members of the U.S. Army Air Service (a predecessor to the U.S. Air Force), were embarking on a daring four-month mission: They were attempting to be the first people to fly around the world. If successful, they would also be the first to cross the Pacific Ocean by plane. At stake was a nation's pride. Although Wilbur and Orville Wright had flown an airplane more than twenty years earlier, back in 1903, the United States had lost the lead in aviation to other nations, especially countries in Europe, that had quickly embraced air transportation. America was falling behind and needed more funding to develop air travel. With this flight, the military hoped to get the American people excited about aviation. To the world, it wanted to prove that the United States could master the air.

However, other countries were not going to let the Americans claim the prize so easily. A British attempt was already under way; the Portuguese and French would begin flights later in April; and the Italians and Argentines would launch their flights in July. The race had begun, and time was important!

The world fliers were excited but also aware of the dangers ahead. Flying was still in its early years, and few landing fields and refueling stations existed around the world. This was not going to be a nonstop flight. The men would need to change the landing gear of their planes, between pontoons (for water

A TICKET TO A PUBLIC AIR SHOW INTENDED TO GENERATE EXCITEMENT FOR THE UPCOMING WORLD FLIGHT.

landings) and wheels (for ground landings), three times during the trip. And they would have to depend on the U.S. Navy and other suppliers to ensure that they would receive the necessary fuel. Navigation would be difficult, because instruments were still simple (there was no radar, for example); pilots relied instead on good visibility. Communication would also be a challenge—none of the planes had radio receivers or transmitters.

Another challenge involved diplomatic relations. The planes would be flying over lands under the control of twenty-five separate governments. Each country or territory required special negotiations. The route that was chosen avoided the Soviet Union, which consisted of present-day Russia and fourteen other countries, because the United States did not recognize the Soviet government. Turkey refused clearance for the flight unless its military officers could inspect the planes. Some countries did not want the fliers traveling over sensitive military areas. Relations with Japan had been antagonistic, and only at the last minute did the Japanese government agree to allow the fliers access.

THE OFFICIAL ARMY AIR SERVICE MAP OF THE WORLD FLIGHT ROUTE.

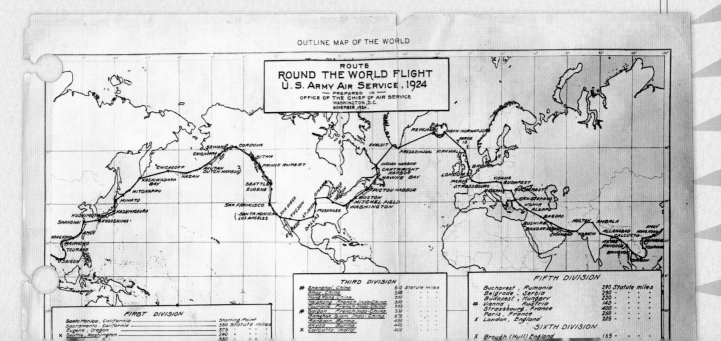

FROM LEFT: WADE, SMITH, MARTIN, AND HARVEY.

As they headed north over the Puget Sound toward Canada, the U.S. airmen encountered thick fog. Poor visibility forced them to drop down to less than one hundred feet above the water. They dodged heavily wooded islands as well as the occasional steamboat plying the waters. There were twenty-foot-high swells, which would make an emergency landing impossible. After a long eight hours through snow squalls and fog banks, the planes reached their first destination: Prince Rupert, British Columbia. The *Seattle* made a stalled landing and dropped onto the water with unusual force. It suffered slight damage. The *Chicago* almost hit some wires that the pilot had not seen. Only the *New Orleans* landed without difficulty. The fourth plane, the *Boston*, arrived an hour later. It had become separated from the rest. Major Frederick Martin in the *Seattle*, the lead plane, had mistakenly identified a photographic plane following them as the *Boston* and so had not waited for it to catch up.

The mayor of Prince Rupert greeted them. "Gentlemen, you have arrived on the worst day we've had in ten years," he proclaimed, referring to the weather. Although the fliers were tired after traveling 650 miles, they graciously attended a dinner that the town held in their honor. This would be the pattern, as communities around the world were eager to wish the intrepid travelers a safe trip and give them local souvenirs. Finally, the dinner party was over, and the airmen collapsed into bed at a local hotel. The very long first day had come to an end.

DOUGLAS WORLD CRUISERS ON THE WATER,
SOMEWHERE IN BRITISH COLUMBIA OR ALASKA.

THE AMERICAN AIRMEN POSE WITH THE MAYOR OF PRINCE RUPERT, BRITISH COLUMBIA, IN FRONT OF THE PRINCE RUPERT HOTEL, APRIL 8, 1924.

More than 400 years ago men first navigated the world. Two years were required, in which many hardships were encountered. Now men travel around the earth by land and water in twenty-eight days. You are going to demonstrate the practicability of making such a voyage by air. Before another 400 years this may be the safest and most comfortable way. Your countrymen will watch your progress with hope and record your success with pride."

—PRESIDENT CALVIN COOLIDGE, MESSAGE TO THE FLIERS, APRIL 2, 1924

PLANNING THE TRIP

APRIL 6, 1924

The eight airmen had beaten many other eager candidates to reach this point. Who wouldn't want to see the world *and* get his name in the record books? More than one hundred officers applied for the opportunity. One applicant, a man named Delmar Dunton, wrote: "The writer wishes to impress again upon the Chief of Air Service his most earnest desire to be included in this expedition, and again makes the urgent request that his case be given the fullest consideration." The top officers of the Army Air Service, including its leader, General Mason Patrick, chose four pilots; the pilots then selected their mechanics. The crews ranged in age from twenty-three to forty-one.

The World Flight trip organizers wanted a high-ranking, experienced pilot to command the expedition, so they selected Major Frederick Martin. He was commander of the Air Service Technical School in Illinois and had about 700 hours of flying time. The other three had their share of flight experience too.

▶ First Lieutenant Lowell Smith learned to fly in Mexico and served in the American military in Europe during World War I, though not in combat. He had experience flying planes to fight forest fires, and competed in several air races. He and a military buddy made the world's first complete refueling of two airplanes in flight, and he established sixteen world records for speed, distance, and duration. Smith had 1,700 hours of flying time.

FIRST LIEUTENANT LOWELL SMITH

▶ First Lieutenant Leigh Wade learned to fly in Canada and trained new combat pilots during World War I. As a test pilot after the war, he made many high-altitude flights and became experienced in aerial photography. Wade came to the flight with 1,500 flight hours.

FIRST LIEUTENANT LEIGH WADE

▶ First Lieutenant Erik Nelson, born in Sweden, served on merchant ships and twice sailed around the world. He came to the United States to be the captain of a racing yacht. After many odd jobs he managed to gain acceptance into the U.S. Army as a mechanic. He eventually gravitated toward aviation. He completed flight training and went on several long-distance flights, including one from New York to Nome, Alaska, and back. Nelson had 1,600 flight hours.

The Army allowed the pilots to choose their partners, the mechanics, from a pool of eight candidates. Major Martin chose Staff Sergeant Alva Harvey, a former student at

FIRST LIEUTENANT ERIK NELSON

a school he had led in Texas. Leigh Wade invited Staff Sergeant Henry Ogden to join him in the *Boston*. At twenty-three, Ogden was the youngest of the world fliers. He liked working on aircraft engines in his spare time. Erik Nelson selected an officer, Lieutenant John Harding, nicknamed "Smiling Jack." Nelson had worked with Harding before and knew that he had a reputation for being able to fix almost anything. Lowell Smith originally selected Technical Sergeant Arthur Turner but ended up taking First Lieutenant Leslie Arnold when Turner became ill before the trip. Arnold had been selected as an alternate pilot, and he was skilled in both flying and fixing.

STAFF SERGEANT HENRY OGDEN

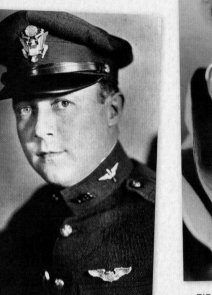

LIEUTENANT JOHN HARDING

FIRST LIEUTENANT LESLIE ARNOLD

The Army planned the expedition carefully, down to the smallest detail. The organizers had to find answers to many questions. Some of the big ones were: What type of aircraft would be able to withstand the rigors of the trip? How many men and aircraft should go? How could the aircraft be refueled? Which direction should they travel? When should they go to take advantage of wind conditions and also avoid seasonal storms? Could they find accurate maps? Would they receive the necessary support from other government agencies? How long would the trip take? How much would it cost?

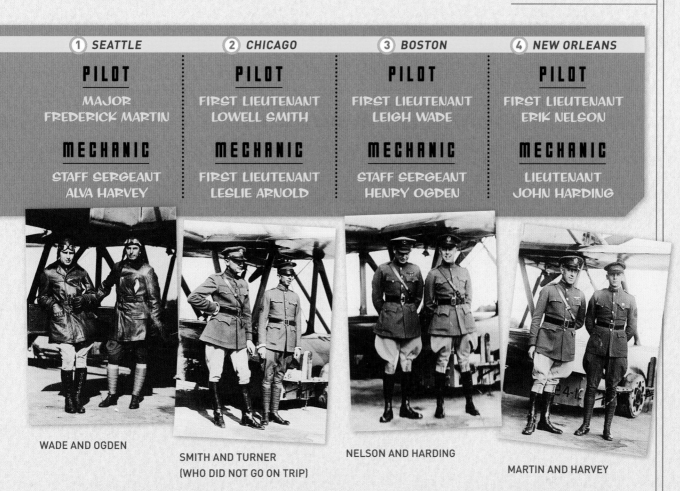

① SEATTLE	② CHICAGO	③ BOSTON	④ NEW ORLEANS
PILOT	**PILOT**	**PILOT**	**PILOT**
MAJOR FREDERICK MARTIN	FIRST LIEUTENANT LOWELL SMITH	FIRST LIEUTENANT LEIGH WADE	FIRST LIEUTENANT ERIK NELSON
MECHANIC	**MECHANIC**	**MECHANIC**	**MECHANIC**
STAFF SERGEANT ALVA HARVEY	FIRST LIEUTENANT LESLIE ARNOLD	STAFF SERGEANT HENRY OGDEN	LIEUTENANT JOHN HARDING

WADE AND OGDEN

SMITH AND TURNER
(WHO DID NOT GO ON TRIP)

NELSON AND HARDING

MARTIN AND HARVEY

Initially, advisers felt the flights should travel eastward, with the prevailing winds. Starting on the West Coast would allow them time to sort out any problems with the aircraft while still in the United States. In the end, though, they decided to send the flights westward, against the winds. Consideration of weather patterns led to this decision. If the trip started in April, the worst weather in Alaska would be past and the fliers would be able to get beyond the Chinese coast before the typhoon season began and also escape the worst of the monsoons in other parts of Asia. Crossing the North Atlantic Ocean at the end of the trip would be safest before the winter weather set in.

What kind of airplane would be just right for an around-the-world flight? There were several requirements: large enough to carry a lot of fuel, fast and nimble enough to face possible emergencies, rugged enough to survive rough oceans and bad weather. Because so few landing fields existed anywhere at the time, certain legs of the trip

THE OFFICIAL PHOTO OF THE AMERICAN FLIERS BEFORE THE FLIGHT (*FROM LEFT*): HARDING, NELSON, WADE, MARTIN, ARNOLD, SMITH, AND LIEUTENANT LECLAIR SCHULTZE, AN ALTERNATE PILOT. THEY'RE WEARING BLACK ARMBANDS IN HONOR OF FORMER PRESIDENT WOODROW WILSON, WHO HAD RECENTLY PASSED AWAY.

would require wheels and others would require pontoons, so the change between the two needed to be easy. The Army finally decided that the planes would be built at the Douglas Aircraft Company factory in Santa Monica, California, and would be a modified version of the Douglas torpedo bomber. The planes were dubbed the Douglas World Cruisers.

Engineers added larger fuel tanks, reinforced the tail section, placed the cockpits closer together for better communication, and added an earth inductor compass—a new, sophisticated means of determining direction. The planes would use two different types of wooden propellers on the trip: walnut when the wheels were installed, oak for pontoons. (Oak was less affected by salt water than other types of wood.) Finally, the Army painted the planes green with yellow wings on top.

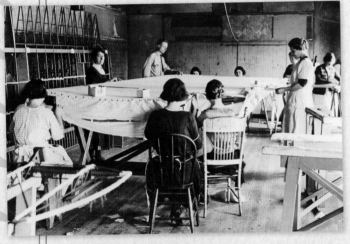

SEAMSTRESSES SEWING A WING.

EMPLOYEES OF THE DOUGLAS AIRCRAFT COMPANY POSING WITH TWO NEW DOUGLAS WORLD CRUISER BIPLANES, SANTA MONICA, CALIFORNIA, JUNE 1923.

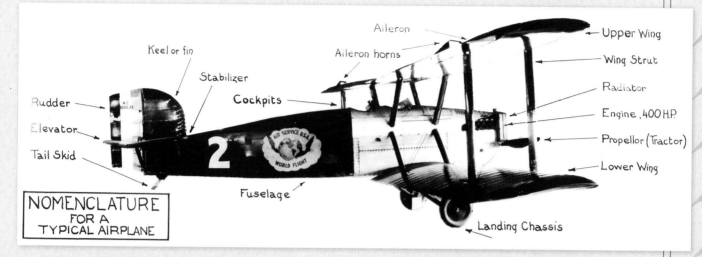

Keel or fin
Stabilizer
Cockpits
Rudder
Elevator
Tail Skid
Fuselage

Aileron
Aileron horns
Upper Wing
Wing Strut
Radiator
Engine, 400 H.P.
Propellor (Tractor)
Lower Wing
Landing Chassis

NOMENCLATURE FOR A TYPICAL AIRPLANE

PARTS OF THE DOUGLAS WORLD CRUISER.

COCKPIT OF THE *CHICAGO*.

The new World Cruisers had a wingspan of fifty feet, two open cockpits, tanks that held 450 gallons of fuel (weighing 2,700 pounds), and capacity for 3,000 additional pounds of crew and supplies. The crews would need to carefully consider everything they brought along; each item had to be worth its weight. For this reason, they made the difficult decision to eliminate radios. (The radios of the time had a maximum transmission range of only about 150 miles.) Because of the weight, they even eliminated parachutes and life preservers! Also, they would document the trip with small, light handheld cameras, not the heavy World War I–era aerial cameras.

The organizers divided the proposed route into six parts, with military officers assigned to guarantee eighteen well-equipped supply and repair depots along the flight path. The duty of each officer was to ensure the quick passage of the fliers through his division and to stay after the flight had passed through to clean up and pay any bills. Of the eighteen supply and repair depots identified along the route, seven were able to undertake major overhauls, such as switching engines or changing pontoons to wheels.

WORLD CRUISER TOOL KIT.

SMITH ARRANGING THE STORAGE COMPARTMENT IN THE FUSELAGE OF THE *CHICAGO*.

A list of items carried in the *Chicago* shows that its crew took eight pounds of books, ten pounds of emergency food, one pound of malted milk tablets, and twelve pounds of thermos bottles. Also on the list was two pounds' worth of "monkeys." At a reception in Los Angeles before the trip, a hotel manager took two stuffed monkeys down from some imitation palm trees and gave them to the fliers as mascots. He promised to pay each pilot fifty dollars for each monkey that was safely returned. Whether good-luck charms or mascots, and despite their added weight, the monkeys would travel around the world with the fliers.

MAGGIE, THE STUFFED MONKEY TAKEN ON THE *BOSTON*.

EACH MAN COULD BRING:

1 FUR-LINED FLIGHT SUIT	2 CHANGES OF UNDERWEAR	1 CAP
1 PAIR OF FUR-LINED GLOVES	2 PAIRS OF LONG WOOLEN STOCKINGS	HANDKERCHIEFS
2 FLANNEL SHIRTS		1 WATERPROOF MATCHBOX
2 PAIRS OF BREECHES	1 PAIR OF HUNTING BOOTS	1 SAFETY RAZOR
		1 TOOTHBRUSH

FIERCE WINDS IN ALASKA

APRIL 10, 1924

After a few days for maintenance, the four planes and their crews left Canada and headed for America's last frontier: the territory of Alaska. (Alaska would not become a state until 1959.) They would spend more than a month there, all the time heading farther west toward their ultimate challenge: the crossing of the Pacific Ocean. If they succeeded, the men would be the first to fly across the ocean to Asia. They chose a route across the North Pacific because they could island-hop most of the way along the Aleutian Islands, a chain of sixty-nine islands stretching westward 1,200 miles from the Alaskan mainland. They hoped that, with support from the U.S. Coast Guard, the stretch of remote territory would not be too challenging. However, no amount of positive thinking could protect them from the screaming winds called "williwaws," as well as from the snowstorms and the raging Bering Sea itself. This would be one of the most difficult parts of the entire trip.

When they left Canada, the *Chicago* was in the lead. Martin, the expedition commander, had decided that they would switch off, giving each pilot the chance to lead the formation. They flew over Ketchikan, where it looked as if the whole town was standing on the wharves and the roofs of buildings to wave as they passed by. They were always encouraged by the friendly crowds. The planes made it to Alaska's first capital, Sitka, where a band and another large crowd welcomed them. The airmen landed on the water and secured the planes at anchor.

WORLD CRUISERS IN FLIGHT, ALASKA.

On the rare sunny days, the fliers enjoyed the extreme beauty of the landscape. One day they spotted their first glaciers. "A river of solid snow and ice—it created quite a feeling of awe," wrote Arnold. In his journal Harding wrote that "the clear deep blue water below, clear sky above, and snow-covered peaks and glaciers on our right were beyond description in beauty and splendor." On clear nights, the scenery was just as spectacular. Arnold wrote, "This evening the moon came out and the effect upon the mountains was beyond description—the most wonderful scenic effects in the world are right here in Alaska, I claim."

The crew quickly established a ritual that they attempted to follow for the rest of the trip: They would prepare the planes for the next day before they went ashore. First, check gas, oil, and water, filling all for the next flight. Next, wash down the engine with kerosene to ensure that dirt and soot did not set. Cover engine sections and cockpits. Check ignition leads and rigging wires, and pontoons for water leakage; flush gasoline strainers; and clean voltage regulators. The process took three to five hours. The men worked with care so that a wrong move wouldn't throw them off balance and into the water. And they quickly learned that the planes needed to be moored tightly to withstand the high winds that could come up suddenly. In Sitka, strong winds blew the *New Orleans* and *Boston* within two feet of each other! The crews watched from the beach, helpless, and fearing certain destruction of the planes. But a forest ranger in a nearby boat acted quickly to prevent a collision.

They landed at Seward, Alaska, on April 13 and left two days later for Chignik, farther along the coast, with the *New Orleans* in the lead. All four planes encountered fierce headwinds, and a thick fog suddenly obscured the *Seattle*, which had dropped to a lower altitude. Fearing that they would run out of fuel if they went back to check on the plane, the others continued, not knowing if the *Seattle* was having mechanical problems or just going slowly. By doing so, they failed to follow their agreed-on plan, which called for the last able plane to circle the one in distress until that plane communicated by pistol signal the seriousness of the trouble. The three other planes landed safely at Chignik and sent word to the Navy to begin a search for the missing aircraft.

ARNOLD (*LEFT*) AND SMITH AND ALL OF THE FLIERS HAD TO BECOME ACCUSTOMED TO BALANCING ON THE PONTOONS.

WORLD CRUISERS AT ANCHOR IN SEWARD, ALASKA, DREW A CROWD.

The *Seattle*'s oil pressure gauge had dropped to zero, but Martin managed a safe landing into a cove in a remote area of Portage Bay. He and Harvey quickly found a three-inch hole in the crankcase and realized they were stuck. After a very cold night spent huddled in the cockpits under the canvas covers, they saw smoke on the horizon; soon two Navy destroyers appeared. A small craft towed the plane to one of the destroyers, where the fliers were given a hot breakfast, and then towed it ten miles to the tiny village of Kanatak. Concerned about the potential for fierce weather, the plane was carefully moved inland to a small pond.

While in Kanatak, Martin and Harvey had their first introduction to williwaws: fierce, sudden, destructive winds that swept down from the mountains in great intensity. Worried that the *Seattle* would be destroyed, the fliers made every attempt to make its lines tight. Even so, at one point they witnessed a williwaw lift the *Seattle* completely above the water and drop it onto its right pontoon. Eventually, all four crews experienced what Arnold referred to as "woolies—a sudden gust of wind of great velocity that comes from most any direction at the most unexpected times and for no apparent reason." He also wrote, "Some of [the] gusts upset rowboats, picked up sheets of water from the surface and took them down the bay, blew boards and planks from the dock, and was [*sic*] generally obnoxious. When walking along they strike you so suddenly and with such force that one can easily be upset."

Martin and Harvey communicated with the other fliers and decided to meet up at the next stop on the itinerary, Dutch Harbor, as soon as possible. A new engine was on the way for the *Seattle*, and they hoped the delay would be only a few days. However, it took them three days in wind and snow to disconnect the bad engine. The new one finally arrived by whaleboat, but high winds prevented any work for two more days. Anxious to be on their way, the *Seattle* crew worked through the night in blowing snow, using gasoline lanterns as a light source. When ice began to form around the pontoons, which could easily damage them, the men of the village quickly helped to break it up. On receiving positive weather reports the following morning, Martin and Harvey took to the air, despite poor visibility at takeoff. They were confident they would leave the poor weather behind.

WILLIWAWS COULD SEVERELY DAMAGE THE WING STRUTS IF THE PLANES WEREN'T ANCHORED PROPERLY, AS THIS IMAGE SHOWS.

WORLD CRUISERS, PULLED UP ON AN ALASKA BEACH TO SECURE THEM FROM HIGH WAVES.

On April 30 the crews waiting in Dutch Harbor for the *Seattle* received word that it had finally departed. They had endured their own encounters with nasty weather and were anxious to move on. Their planes had gotten loose from the moorings and required an intensive effort to secure them, with the aid of sailors from the Coast Guard cutter *Haida*. Arnold described the scene:

A gale suddenly swept in from the Arctic Ocean and the waves dashed so high up [on the beach] that they tore the planes loose . . . It was dark as the nethermost pit . . . snowing like the dickens, the wind was howling, and the waves were booming on the beach . . . We were rushing about wildly and wading around in the water trying to get hold of the planes before they were swept into the bay. Some of us floundered in that icy water right up to our necks, and worked for two hours and a half. It was after midnight with the weather near zero before we managed to pull the planes higher on the beach, away from the threatening seas, and had them safely secured . . . When we got back to the trader's house that night, we were so cold that we couldn't even unbutton our coats.

While in the Aleutian Islands, the crews relied on the *Haida*'s radio equipment and various naval radio stations along the route for communication. Prior to the flight, the organizers had also made arrangements for the different fish canneries en route to send messages to Dutch Harbor with the time that the planes passed overhead.

On April 30, however, no messages came in to alert the three waiting crews that the *Seattle* had passed any of these checkpoints. It became clear pretty quickly that once again something was wrong. A massive search was begun, with Coast Guard ships and small motorboats from the canneries, as well as two dog teams going inland. After a week passed with no signs of the *Seattle* crew, the search intensified. There was nothing the three crews could do but wait.

Despite the stress of not knowing whether their friends were alive, the two-week stay in Dutch Harbor allowed the three crews to rest up. They spent the days writing letters home, sleeping, reading, playing bridge, and even shoveling the snow off the tennis courts and hitting seven sets of tennis. "Rather cold on the hands but exhilarating!" wrote Arnold. They also set up a temporary laboratory to develop the film they had shot on their trip up to that point. And they celebrated Russian Easter, attending a four-hour-long midnight service at the Russian Orthodox Church. Arnold wrote that the Aleuts stood for the service but provided benches for the fliers.

WHILE THE AIRMEN WAITED FOR ORDERS TO CONTINUE THEIR FLIGHT, THERE WAS TIME FOR RELAXATION. PLAYING IN THE SNOW ARE (*FROM LEFT*) OGDEN, HARDING (SEATED), NELSON, SMITH, AND WADE.

Arnold wrote on April 30 that, for the first time since leaving Seattle, a day had passed without a snowstorm. He also commented, "I've heard of 'bad weather' many times but unless a person has been in [Alaska] in April they haven't seen anything at all . . . I think we all are fed up on [*sic*] Alaskan weather." The crews in Dutch Harbor were restless by now, and though concerned for their missing *Seattle* comrades, they wanted to continue with the trip. Yet the flight's leader, Major Martin, was missing.

4

DISASTER ON THE MOUNTAIN

APRIL 30, 1924

Martin and Harvey set out in the *Seattle* to fly over what they had been told was low ground. In an effort to avoid fog directly in their path, Martin steered the plane overland, since he spotted water in the distance. The fliers were always alert to the danger of going too far inland with pontoons, because there was no guarantee they could find a body of water on which to land. Then, in the midst of the "low ground," a mountain appeared! There was no way to avoid it, and they crashed. However, it was a decent crash, as crashes go, and not a rough jolt.

Fortunately, the only injury was a slight cut over Martin's eye and a bloody nose. But the plane was now a crumpled heap of parts, and they knew right away that their journey was over. Survival became their top priority. They were stranded on

THE WRECKAGE OF THE *SEATTLE* NEAR PORT MOLLER, ALASKA.

a mountain in bad weather, with miles of rugged, snowy landscape around them. They had no idea how close the nearest human settlement was, and certainly no clue which direction to head. Their food supply consisted of four sandwiches, a dozen malted milk tablets, and two thermos bottles of concentrated food in liquid form. Martin's compass had broken, but Harvey found that he had a small, though often unreliable, card compass. In addition, they had a map—but where was their location on it? The airmen estimated that they were ten miles from the Pacific coast, with a mountain range in the way, but they did not really know for sure.

They set out and soon became confused by the snow glare and the fog. Vision was limited to a few feet. They returned to the plane wreckage the first night, since they didn't think they could find shelter anywhere else. They knew that a heavy fog could persist for days, and they realized their situation was dire. Harvey later recalled that "to expect outside rescue was pure folly. The matter of survival was entirely up to us, so we made an agreement and shook hands on it. We would start for the coast, never to return to the airplane again. Saying 'Farewell *Seattle*, we regret leaving you here wrecked and battered,' we walked away."

Martin and Harvey quickly settled into a steady pace, with one man in front and the other about one hundred feet behind. They began following a creek, hoping it would lead to the Bering Sea, but then changed their minds because their map indicated no villages or canneries on the Bering Sea side of the mountains. Next, the weary fliers climbed the summit of a mountain and then headed toward a lake in the distance, with the hope that a trapper might be in the area. Their food consumed, they managed to kill two small birds called ptarmigans with an Army pistol and cooked them on a small fire.

FLIGHT COMMANDER MAJOR MARTIN AND STAFF SERGEANT HARVEY AFTER THEIR TREK OUT OF THE MOUNTAINS.

Finding no signs of habitation on the lake the following day, Martin and Harvey decided to follow a stream from the lake, suspecting that it would guide them through the mountains. Walking in dry creek beds, they made good time and eventually came to a large body of water, where they found a small cabin; it was filled with supplies and had a small stove with wood and an oil heater. All evidence suggested that it had been occupied within the previous twenty-four hours.

Martin later talked about one of the nights when he and Harvey camped in a thicket: "It was a terrible night. I, myself, was snow-blind and Harvey was breaking trail all day. Both of us had a completely exhausted feeling whenever we stopped. The snow was four feet deep and there were bear tracks as large as those of elephants, the largest I ever saw."

A carton containing cans of condensed milk was addressed to the Port Moller Cannery. They located the spot on a map and estimated that it was twenty-five miles away. Walking along the beach, along what they decided was the Bering Sea, they made excellent progress and were thrilled to finally see the signs of Port Moller: a radio mast and smokestacks. They would live!

Martin sent a message to the chief

of the Air Service: "Ship [a term commonly used for planes] a total wreck. Existence due to concentrated food and nerve." News of their survival spread quickly, and American newspapers reported it with large headlines. A fisheries company steamer took them to Bellingham, Washington, where they were greeted by more than a thousand well-wishers. In Washington, D.C., General Patrick, the man in charge of the expedition, sent a radiogram acknowledging that the Army Air Service still wanted Martin to command the trip; he had already started thinking about how Martin and Harvey could rejoin the flight. Martin took some time to reflect and responded: "While there is nothing I should like better than to rejoin the flight and again take command, by that time a considerable part of it will have been accomplished without me. In fairness to Lieutenant Smith, who succeeded me in command, I think he should so continue and himself bring the flight back to the United States." Years later, Harvey wrote, "The experience gained, the hazards faced, and the few hardships endured proved invaluable in the years since. I have always cherished the memory of those few months. A strong bond of friendship and mutual respect was formed between Major Martin and me which has endured throughout the years."

THE *ATLANTA CONSTITUTION*'S FRONT PAGE TELLS THE GOOD NEWS THAT MARTIN AND HARVEY ARE SAFE.

5

FIRST ACROSS THE PACIFIC

MAY 2, 1924

S till wondering about the fate of their colleagues Martin and Harvey, the other fliers finally received the order they had been waiting for: Proceed! Lieutenant Lowell Smith would be the flight's new commander, and the group was to head to Japan at the earliest possible moment. The following day they took off, flying west to islands farther out in the archipelago.

Once again, bad weather stopped them. Would they never get out of Alaska? Arnold wrote, "The Aleutians have but two kinds of weather it seems, bad and worse." An old trapper told Wade, "We have only two seasons

[*FROM LEFT*] NELSON, SMITH, HARDING, AND ARNOLD, RESTED AND READY TO GO.

here, this winter and next winter." They carefully monitored the weather ahead, because while it might be clear where they were, they could easily head into problems.

VIEW OF TWO WORLD CRUISERS, WITH THE *HAIDA* IN THE DISTANCE, ATKA, ALASKA.

The fliers had already learned about the challenges of flying in all kinds of weather. Thick fog or snowfall could cause visibility to drop unexpectedly, requiring the planes to fly just feet above the water. Arnold wrote that in such conditions "everything was one color and we might have almost been flying in total darkness. Sometimes we flew so low that our pontoons almost dragged on the water." Their fur-lined flight suits and gloves, and their helmets and goggles, shielded them from some of the weather, but the open cockpits did not protect them from raindrops, which one pilot described as feeling "like lead shot being thrown into our faces and against our hands."

Finally, the weather cleared, and in eight hours the three remaining planes safely traveled the 555 miles to Chichagof Harbor on Attu Island, the last stop in Alaska. Arnold described the place as having three wooden houses and a number of "barrabas," or huts of grass and sod with a floor space of about eight by ten feet, in which six to eight people lived. The village had a population of fifty-nine Aleuts and was the westernmost settlement in the United States.

CLOSE-UP VIEW OF A "BARRABAS" SOD HUT ON ATTU ISLAND, ALEUTIAN ISLANDS.

The *Haida* arrived with the good news that Martin and Harvey were safe. Wade wrote, "It was heartening news to all of us . . . but the flight was hardly started. Who might be next? I shut my mind to the thought, tried to start each new day with yesterday wiped from the slate."

While in Chichagof Harbor, the crews received a letter that emphasized the urgency of avoiding delay. Colonel L. E. Broome, advance man for the British around-the-world flight, had written to wish them well. They thought this gesture thoughtful and a demonstration of good sportsmanship. But it reminded them that they were in a race for national pride. The British flight had left London and within one month had reached Karachi, India (now in Pakistan). The Portuguese and French flights had also begun. The prestige of American aviation was on the line.

At 5:00 A.M. on May 15, the airmen awoke to a report of clear weather ahead. This was the big day, when they hoped to be the first across the Pacific by air. They were ready. The night before, on the *Haida*, they had dined on a turkey dinner and, Arnold wrote later, had been "given a real treat in the form of a bath—I don't dare mention when we had our last one." This crossing would probably be the most difficult part of their entire trip. They took off without problems and circled low over the *Haida*, which was "rolling and tossing like a cork." The crewmen were out on deck, each holding on for dear life with one hand and waving with the other. This particular location, where the North Pacific Ocean meets the Bering Sea, has been called the roughest area of what is considered one of the roughest bodies of water in the world.

The planes soon crossed the International Date Line; west of it, the date was one day later. Instead of aiming straight for Japan, the fliers had decided to make a fuel

A U.S. COAST GUARD CUTTER SIMILAR TO THE *HAIDA*.

stop at the Komandorski Islands, a territory of the Soviet Union—a country the United States did not have diplomatic relations with. Since the U.S. Army had not made prior arrangements with the Soviet government, the fliers were making a risky move. While they wouldn't be on the Soviet mainland, they would be in Soviet waters. What kind of reception would they receive?

The three crews flew for three hours without any sight of land, the first real test of their navigational skills. They began looking for Copper Island (now known as Medny Island), the easternmost of the Komandorski Islands, only nine miles by one mile—

THE SOVIET MEN WHO MET WITH THE FLIERS HEAD BACK TO SHORE. THIS PHOTO WAS TAKEN FROM THE *EIDER*.

a dot in the vast ocean. With relief they spotted it on the horizon, along with the *Eider*, a U.S. Bureau of Fisheries support boat they had arranged to meet. The *Eider* carried fuel for them.

As the planes rendezvoused with the *Eider*, a Soviet boat with a number of men, two in uniform and carrying rifles, left the small island and rowed out to them. The men asked the fliers' business and apologized that they could not invite the Americans ashore until they had obtained permission from the Soviet authorities in Moscow. The fliers assured the men that they were passing through and would stay on the *Eider* only one night. The Soviet men returned to the island but later confirmed that permission had not been granted to the Americans to join them. Fortunately, the weather allowed the fliers to take off early the following morning.

During the next segment of the trip, the flight would receive support from the U.S. Navy. Several Navy ships were heading to position off the Japanese coast to greet the fliers. In the Kurile Islands in northern Japan (now controlled by Russia), the *Ford* waited.

Among its passengers was a determined Associated Press newspaper reporter, Linton Wells, who was based in Tokyo. He wanted the story badly and paced the deck straining to hear the sound of engines above. Suddenly, he heard it! The three World Cruisers appeared. He quickly filed a report and achieved his scoop:

> The first flight in aviation history was made in this ice-fenced and remotely situated bay bordering the Arctic when six United States airmen landed here at 11:30 this morning, completing the most perilous undertaking ever attempted and winning [for] America the honor of being the first to cross the Pacific by air.
>
> Fighting their way through a world of obstructions, bucking cold, blustering Arctic winds, thick, almost impenetrable fogs, blinding snowstorms, icy rains, receiving as a result lacerated skins, all of which they beat and retard in every turn, the six airmen in landing here added another laurel wreath to the long list of America's accomplishments.

Wells wanted his American newspaper readers to feel proud, and he had good reason. The flight demonstrated to the world that the Pacific could be crossed, that Asia and America were now closer than ever, and that American aviation had earned credibility on the world stage. Congratulations began to pour in, and even the Japanese minister of war sent his welcome and good wishes. Arnold conveyed the general feeling of the crew when he wrote, "We are all greatly relieved to have the Aleutian Islands and the Pacific behind us." Since the seas were too rough to allow refueling, the men could relax—they played cards and got haircuts. The next day they would be in Japan, a culture completely unfamiliar to them.

COLORFUL JAPAN

MAY 17, 1924

For the next two and a half weeks, the world fliers made their way south along the coast of Japan. Since American relations with the Japanese government were not exactly warm, they did not know what to expect. While in Japan, the fliers planned to get their planes ready for the warmer climates ahead. They were once again in a populated area, and Arnold commented that it was a "nice change to pass villages, boats and see people after desolation." They were still island-hopping: the country of Japan consists of more than 6,000 mostly small islands.

The fliers' introduction to Japanese culture began when they landed in Hitokappu Bay and promptly got fogged

FISHING BOATS ALONG THE COAST OF JAPAN.

in for three days. The U.S. destroyer *Pope* provided their sleeping accommodations. They went ashore to the village of Yanketo and visited the home of an elderly man who gave them tea. "We were fascinated with the village, with its tiny houses that looked like eggshells," said Wade. They also saw small, shaggy-haired horses, unlike those they were familiar with in the United States.

ARRIVING AT LAKE KASUMIGAURA, 50 MILES FROM TOKYO.

Two Japanese destroyers had welcomed them to Japan, and one afternoon the Japanese crews invited the fliers to witness a sumo match, which Arnold described as "better than a circus." He wrote a lengthy passage in his journal:

The participants strip to a breech clout and the idea seems to be to force the other outside of the ring. The men were wonderful physical specimens and I have new respect for their strength and prowess. The wrestlers are prone to pose, stamp their feet, and stretch their muscles—and all in a manner that amused us greatly but to them is a native custom. Another custom is that of throwing salt into the arena at the feet of their opponent to drive away any evil spirits that may be with said opponent. The referee is also a very important personage, had full control, and armed with a fan and in his bare feet; his decisions are never contested.

Afterward, the Japanese officers served cakes and wine. Impressed with their hospitality, the fliers returned the invitation and entertained the Japanese with motion pictures on an American ship.

On May 22, the weather cooperated and the fliers departed for the Tokyo area, stopping briefly at Minato. Arnold wrote that he saw his first smoking volcano, and he described the beauty of the landscape: "many small villages tucked away in the valleys, lots of rice paddys with their irrigation lay outs, some private estates with well-kept grounds." Minato, the largest city they had visited since Seattle (and now a district within Tokyo), put on an elaborate reception. Hundreds of schoolchildren waved American flags, and men fired rockets and fireworks in welcome. Since they were behind schedule, Smith decided they could not afford the time to go ashore and asked the American advance officer, Lieutenant Clifford Nutt, to convey their regrets.

CROWD ASSEMBLED TO WATCH THE DEPARTURE OF THE WORLD CRUISERS, KUSHIMOTO, JAPAN.

If the Americans were surprised by the reception in Minato, an even bigger one awaited them at Lake Kasumigaura, home of the Japanese Navy about fifty miles from Tokyo, the country's capital. A crowd of 10,000 people welcomed them, along with a large press corps eager for stories of their journey thus far. As they looked out at the crowd, they noticed bright, traditional Japanese dress. Arnold wrote that "the native costumes of course attracted our attention— for variety of color they are unbeatable."

Their stay in the Tokyo area lasted ten days. In the Aleutian Islands they had often slept in shacks, "where we made our beds on boxes to keep the rats from running over us." Now they stayed in the officers' club and had private rooms and baths, a special cook to prepare American food, and three orderlies to care for their needs. While excited to see the sights of Tokyo, the men had work to do. Their priority was overhauling the planes, a week's worth of work. This included changing the engines, pontoons, and propellers, as well as installing larger radiators for warmer climates. They did the work themselves, though Japanese mechanics stood at hand. The fliers noticed that the Japanese took a lot of photographs of every part of the planes and made precise drawings, careful to take exact measurements.

A new challenge threatened the planes. It wasn't williwaws this time but the heavy boat traffic on the lake, which could result in collisions with the aircraft. The crews were required to maintain constant vigilance after an unmanned boat drifted toward the *Chicago* and almost rammed it.

Their work went beyond preparing the planes. They were suddenly goodwill ambassadors for the United States, with diplomatic duties. While they worked hard, they also played hard. The Japanese military and other officials had organized elaborate events for the fliers, to be spread out over two weeks. However, Smith was well aware that the flight was already thirty-one days behind the planned schedule. They needed to finish the work and get on their way. He politely insisted that the ceremonies be compressed into two days.

CHANGING A MOTOR IN JAPAN.

One evening the Japanese admiral hosted them at a dinner, complete with geishas, which Arnold later described in his diary: "We were welcomed by a crowd of Japanese maids in flowered kimonos, it seemed as though we had stepped into the pages of a storybook. The pretty geisha girls were there to serve and entertain us—demure, delightful, laughing-eyed . . . Each geisha devotes herself exclusively to the man she is waiting on, removes the various courses, brings others, lights his cigarettes as he reclines on his cushion, fills his little cup with warm sake, and initiates him into the mystery of using chopsticks."

SMITH RECEIVES A SOUVENIR FROM THE TOWN OF KUSHIMOTO.

THE SILVER CITY OF KUSHIMOTO MEDAL (*FRONT AND BACK*) THAT WAS PRESENTED TO THE WORLD CRUISER CREWS.

The fliers did have time to visit Tokyo, stayed at the Imperial Hotel, and had drivers and translators at the ready for them. They toured the sights and attended receptions, luncheons, dinners, teas, and dances. They met the American ambassador, the Japanese minister of war and the Navy, and Prince Kuni of the royal family. They received gifts and awards, medals and silver bowls. The entire diplomatic corps gathered at a dance and reception in their honor. The president of Tokyo University gave "a most brilliant" speech at another dinner held for them, praising their accomplishment "of being the first of men to connect the shores of the Pacific Ocean through the sky." Looking back at their stay, Arnold wrote that they "had a time that passes all attempts to describe. When it was all over we were in a daze." They also experienced three earthquakes!

THE FLIERS RELAX AT THE NAVAL AIR STATION AT KASUMIGAURA. NELSON CONFERS WITH A JAPANESE NAVAL OFFICER ABOUT THE ROUTE TO KUSHIMOTO.

Everywhere they went, including Kasumigaura, Kushimoto, and Kagoshima, crowds followed them, along with reporters and photographers. In Alaska it had seemed they were on a personal journey, but now, on another continent, they realized the significance of the flight. Wade said it best—that "it was no longer just a personal adventure. The United States could not be let down. We started watching ourselves and our actions on the ground. Diplomatic correctness became as important as our aerial skills."

MECHANICAL TROUBLE IN INDOCHINA

JUNE 4–5, 1924

On June 4, the *Boston* and the *New Orleans* left Japan, finally on their way across the China Sea to Shanghai, China; the *Chicago*, unable to take off successfully with them, followed on the next day. This trip was another first: No one had ever flown across the China Sea.

The flight was a month behind schedule. The American fliers were well aware that they were still in a race. A few days earlier they had received word that the French pilot, Captain Georges Pelletier d'Oisy, had crashed and destroyed his plane, causing the French to bow out of the competition. The British crew, led by Archibald Stuart Charles Stuart MacLaren, had also crashed, but there was a backup craft. However, the second plane wasn't near the crash site, and the British military refused to help, because the crew was doing this without government support. The British crew was shocked when the Americans offered to ask the U.S. military to transport the spare plane to them—and even more surprised when the military agreed. One exclaimed, "That's the finest bit of sportsmanship I've ever heard of!" And as far as the world fliers knew, the Portuguese

WORLD CRUISERS AT ANCHOR IN SHANGHAI, CHINA, SURROUNDED BY JUNKS AND SAMPANS.

flight was continuing its journey. The round-the-world race was still on!

The arrival in China marked still another first for the American mission—the first time an aircraft had reached China from the United States. The challenge in Chinese waters was again boat traffic—sampans, steamships, and junks were everywhere. The crews received a large welcome from hundreds of Americans and Europeans and from a delegation led by the chief of the Chinese Air Force. Despite the warm greeting, the fliers were tired and wished they could work on their planes instead of having to talk with people.

They took to the air two days later, this time dodging even more boat traffic and needing to make several takeoff attempts. Heading southwest along the Chinese coast, they again had the support of the U.S. Navy. Several destroyers had steamed ahead with fuel and were ready to meet them at predetermined spots and provide lodging. The *Chicago* was having problems; several days earlier its crew discovered that a metal strip had been torn off the bottom of one of its pontoons. The fliers spent a good part of a day in the water, diving down to fix the problem. "Swimming around under the pontoons was a job for a mermaid," said Smith,

THE *CHICAGO* BEING HOISTED BY CRANE IN HONG KONG.

"not for an airman. We swallowed quarts of water." Now one of the pontoons was leaking badly. They landed near the Standard Oil Company dock in Hong Kong and, with help from an oil company agent, managed to find a portable crane. The crane lifted the plane from the water, allowing them to install a new pontoon that had been brought previously by a Navy destroyer.

Two days after that, the fliers departed China and reached French Indochina (landing in what is now Vietnam). The French governor-general gave them a reception. There they learned that the two Portuguese pilots flying around the world had crashed in India—but also that Britain's Royal Air Force (RAF) had given them a new plane and they were continuing on their way. The British crew, meanwhile, was still waiting for its replacement plane.

On June 11, the American fliers soared into the air after a challenging takeoff. The warm climate's still air created calm water, especially in the early morning, and this made it hard to take off. An airplane flying from calm water must overcome a suction-like force that makes it difficult for the pontoons to break free of the smooth surface. A few ripples or small waves make all the difference. The fliers had to taxi back and forth to create ripples in the water, which sometimes took hours to produce. Only then could they climb into the air. Several times they decided to lessen the fuel load to make the planes lighter for lift—but then they needed to make an extra fuel stop later.

If Smith and Arnold thought the *Chicago*'s troubles were fixed, they were wrong. The engine began to overheat, and Smith quickly landed in a calm lagoon. They filled the radiator with water and hoped the problem was solved,

but twenty minutes later the engine overheated again. They found another lagoon and landed, worried that a fire might erupt at any moment. They quickly assessed the trouble and realized that the engine could not be repaired. They were stranded. The *Boston* and *New Orleans* also landed, and their colleagues gave them all the food and water available and promised to return with a new engine.

PEOPLE AROUND THE WORLD WERE CURIOUS ABOUT THE WORLD CRUISERS AND WANTED TO GET CLOSE TO THE PLANES.

When their friends were out of sight, Smith and Arnold looked at their surroundings. The water around them was filled with fishermen checking hundreds of traps— and with crocodiles that occasionally rose to the surface to survey the action. The locals quickly lost any inhibition and surrounded the plane, attempting to climb onto the pontoons. Since a boat could gouge the pontoons and sink the plane, the fliers tried desperately to keep the locals away.

The day grew hot, and Smith and Arnold soon drank all the water they had. Some people who spoke French came along and warned them not to drink any water the natives offered them; it could cause dysentery and other illness in anyone not accustomed to it. Arnold took an empty container, borrowed a dugout, and went in search of a freshwater spring. While he was gone, Smith grew desperately thirsty. Finally, he gave in, drinking some water given to him by a local.

The *Boston* and *New Orleans* continued on to Tourane (present-day Da Nang, Vietnam), the next stop on the itinerary. There they devised a plan of action: A U.S. Navy ship would deliver a new engine from Saigon (now Ho Chi Minh City); in the meantime, Nelson would return to the *Chicago* with supplies, while Wade, Harding, and Ogden would perform maintenance on the *Boston* and *New Orleans*. The closest city to the *Chicago* was Hue. It took Nelson and his party three hours to travel there by automobile. Beyond Hue, traveling through thick jungles by sampan and on foot was an adventure. Nelson wrote:

It was pitch dark, not even a star. How the natives could find their way around the bends in that stream on such an inky night was beyond me . . . This is a great tiger country, and the Annamites [the local residents of the province of Annam] live in mortal terror of "Master Stripes." They also have a wholesome respect for crocodiles. Before we got into their sampan they threw a little cooked rice into the river and offered up a prayer to the spirits of the night, imploring them to protect us. We proceeded in single file, and what impressed me most was the multitude of little shrines all along the way where the men said their prayers and left offerings for the tigers and other forest friends. Every traveler who goes this way leaves a banana or a bit of rice on these altars. There were shrines every five minutes, and occasionally we passed a good-sized temple. On both sides of the trail there was dense jungle that could only be penetrated by cutting your way through with an ax.

At about 2:00 A.M. Nelson's party found the *Chicago*, with Arnold stretched out on the wing, and they had a joyous reunion. The locals arranged for several men from a nearby village to tow the plane the twenty miles to Hue, using three sampans. It must have been quite a sight: a parade, including a chieftain with a boatload of women keeping him supplied with water, tea, and bananas, as well as various houseboats along for the ride. Arnold later regretted that they didn't have a camera, because "the pictures of our outfit would have been worth a mint." He wrote:

> Our trip took us up through a narrow river— the banks were covered with dense tropical foliage, many native villages with their thatched huts and innumerable natives were on the banks watching us go by. We saw elephants with great tusks plodding along with huge loads on their backs,

DURING THEIR TRAVELS, THE AMERICAN FLIERS SAW MANY SIGHTS THAT WERE COMPLETELY NEW TO THEM, SUCH AS ELEPHANTS AT WORK IN TEAK YARDS NEAR RANGOON, BURMA.

water buffalo laying in the water with only their nose and horns sticking out, sampans of all sorts and descriptions, and natives garbed (and without garbs) in all ways. The experiences and sights of today we both agree will never be forgotten and yet we could never describe to anyone. They must be seen to be appreciated.

Early the next morning in Hue, Smith and Arnold got to work removing the engine, but the heat was so intense that by 10:00 A.M. their metal tools were too hot to pick up. They could not touch the engine or any other metal parts of the plane and began to feel ill. Arnold wrote later, "I'm sure God never meant it to be as hot as it was here today." They cooled off in the home of a local French teacher, who invited them to join him on a tiger hunt. He was disappointed when they turned down his offer because of a lack of time. As soon as the new engine showed up, they would have work to do. Finally, Nelson arrived with the replacement engine, mechanics Harding and Ogden, and some American sailors. Then the five airmen worked almost eight hours, using a bridge to suspend a sling to raise and lower the old and new engines. Arnold wrote of the huge crowd of locals watching the procedure: "they were certainly treated to a sight of American ingenuity and progressiveness." In an impressive display of teamwork, the crew replaced the engine and was ready to go only seventy-one hours after the initial landing on the lagoon.

FROM LEFT: WADE, SMITH, AND OGDEN INSPECT A LIBERTY 12 ENGINE.

AMERICAN SAILORS, UNDER THE SUPERVISION OF SMITH AND ARNOLD, HELPED CHANGE THE *CHICAGO*'S ENGINE AT HUE.

Before leaving Hue, Smith and Arnold took a rickshaw ride to see the grounds of the Annamite king's palace and an old Buddhist temple. They also noticed the native graveyards, each tomb a round mound surrounded by a dry moat, looking like concentric circles from the air. They were also amazed by the numbers of fish traps in the lagoons. As Arnold noted, "A fish hasn't a chance in their waters."

The *Chicago* rejoined the other planes in Tourane. On June 16, after seven hours of smooth flying over swamps, rice fields, and many water buffalo (which were always spooked by the planes, much to the fliers' amusement), they landed in Saigon, "the Paris of the East," the southernmost point of their entire flight. They stayed for two days to perform routine maintenance and to briefly explore this busy city, with its European-style buildings and sidewalk cafés.

Next stop: Bangkok, Siam (now Thailand). There they took time to spend a half day sightseeing around the capital city. Arnold wrote: "We saw the white elephants, the [king's] palace, throne halls, a miniature of the famous ruins near here that were recently discovered, and visited a couple of temples. In one was a huge sleeping Buddha, a gigantic thing. We also visited the King's temple and here saw the famous jade Buddha with the diamond in the forehead, reputed to be worth well over a million dollars." They were impressed with Siam. Arnold added that "the Siamese are a very keen race—smart, courteous, kind and very likeable. It would be most interesting to stay here long enough to see more of the country." The white sandy beaches and waving coconut palms had caught their attention from the air, but they needed to keep going.

1 THE FLIERS GO SIGHTSEEING IN BANGKOK.

2 TEMPLES AT BANGKOK.

Each stop offered the lure of exotic sites—plus the hot, sticky air of the tropics. There were no large crowds now, only curious locals and, again, busy rivers full of boat traffic. By this time the flight was way behind schedule, and on their way to Tavoy, Burma (now officially Myanmar), they faced yet another decision, a risky option that could save them two days of travel time. They could take a shortcut across the Malay Peninsula, over the Malaysian jungle. There would be no access to water for landing, and engine failure would mean disaster. Smith decided to risk it, and the planes flew directly to Tavoy. It was a bumpy ride over 4,000-foot-high mountains, but they encountered no problems and arrived safely. The destroyer *Sicard* awaited them, and they refueled and took off in a sudden storm, because there was no sheltered place to wait it out.

Their next landing, at Rangoon (now officially Yangon) in Burma, was another exercise in navigating around major boat traffic, this time on the Irrawaddy River. Once on the water, Smith turned the *Chicago* sharply to avoid a collision with a boat—and Arnold fell in the river. Not realizing that Arnold, who was wearing heavy flying clothes, was in the water, Smith taxied away. He soon realized his error, however, and went back to save his colleague. All three planes were finally safely on the water—but then the fliers noticed a large riverboat under full sail heading directly toward them. A nearby American sailor managed to jump on the boat and turn it, but not soon enough. The boat hit the *New Orleans*, causing major damage. It took five days to complete repairs, so the fliers lost any time they had gained by the shortcut.

Smith was not ready to fly anyway, because he had come down with dysentery caused by the water he had drunk while stranded in the lagoon earlier. They sent for a British doctor, who confined him to bed for several days.

A MEDICAL KIT LIKE THOSE CARRIED ON EACH DOUGLAS WORLD CRUISER.

The race was still on, and the fliers were sensitive to any time lost. The British flight had received its backup plane and was continuing eastward. At one point, the Americans, traveling west, flew over the British plane without realizing it. The British, who had stopped briefly to wait out a storm, heard the Americans but did not see them because of poor visibility. The Portuguese, on the other hand, were out of the race. After flying 11,000 miles, they had again crashed, this time near Hong Kong a few days earlier, which ended their quest.

Over the next few days the Americans made their way across Burma toward India. They crossed the dangerous deltas of the Ganges and the Brahmaputra Rivers. This vast, remote land was also known for its tigers and crocodiles—animals they didn't want to encounter. Smith later said:

We now had one of the most dangerous stretches in the world ahead of us. The deltas of two of the largest rivers on earth lie between Chittatong [*sic*] and Calcutta. The Ganges and the Brahmaputra, each of which is about the size of the Mississippi, join in central Bengal. But not only do they form one main stream, the Hoogil [*sic*], which is often over ten miles wide, but hundreds of other channels spread out fanlike and empty into the bay. Between these channels and countless creeks are sandbars, dense jungle, and mangrove swamps. Here and there are a few villages nearly smothered by the luxuriant vegetation. But the jungle is inhabited mainly by enormous numbers of deer, tigers, and monkeys, while the murky backwaters swarm with crocodiles. A large part of the region is virgin. Our maps were of but little use on the flight . . . The only precaution we could take was to fly fairly high in order to always be within gliding distance of a body of water of some description in case of engine trouble. But even to come down safely on one of those channels would simply have been the start of one's trouble . . . search parties in boats might hunt a month without finding you.

THE HEAT OF INDIA

JUNE 26, 1924

Thankfully, they made it to Calcutta (now Kolkata), India, with no trouble. Calcutta had been designated a major repair center for the trip, and now a large amount of work would begin. The fliers would exchange the pontoons for wheels and continue on to western Europe, flying over land. Other work included inspecting every inch of the planes, repainting the fuselage fabric, and installing larger engine radiators for the desert heat ahead. They also hired a tailor to sew tropical uniforms, better suited for the heat, and took their clothes to be laundered.

OGDEN, HARDING, AND WADE WORE SHORT
PANTS TO STAY COOL.

The Americans were surprised that in India monkeys were as common as birds in the United States. And cows, considered sacred in Hindu religion, wandered the city at will. When one lay down under a plane's wing, Ogden had to twist its tail to make it move. A large crowd of locals watched the men work on the planes day and night, and fifty policemen were present to provide crowd control.

Calcutta from the air, with its countless mills and jute factories, its mammoth docks, its rows and rows of ocean going vessels, ferries and native river craft, its handsome residential quarters, its great common in the center of the city, with a magnificent white marble domed palace at one end, its crowded streets and modern office buildings, made it one of the most impressive sights of the orient," said Smith.

1 WHILE FLYING OVER CALCUTTA, THE MEN SPOTTED A RAJAH'S PALACE ON THE GANGES RIVER.

2 THE FLIERS WERE FETED ALL ALONG THEIR ROUTE. HERE THEY'RE WELCOMED AT A BANQUET GIVEN BY THE AMERICAN LEGION POST OF CALCUTTA.

As they prepared to leave Calcutta, the Americans received an odd request. Linton Wells, the Associated Press reporter who had reported on their trip since the beginning, had caught up with them again. Befriending the fliers, he offered to help with repair work during the stop. Now he pleaded for them to take him along on the next leg of their trip! It was against Army regulations to carry passengers; in addition, the heat

ASSOCIATED PRESS REPORTER LINTON WELLS.

required that the planes be kept as light as possible. Still, the men knew that his articles could generate valuable publicity and goodwill back home.

Smith was initially against it, but Wade was willing to let Wells squeeze in beside Ogden in the *Boston*. Everyone acknowledged that Wells would be extra help. Smith had broken a rib in a fall and was moving slowly. He agreed to request permission for the journalist to accompany them. When they didn't get an answer from their superiors back home by the time they were ready to leave, the fliers made their own decision: Wells would join them.

"Ogden and I were jammed into the cockpit like a pair of Siamese twins, and during the six hours and thirty minutes' flight to Allahabad neither of us could move an inch," Wells later wrote.

Ogden was miserable: "If it hadn't been for the glorious scenery of the snow-capped Himalayas, I believe I should have thrown Wells overboard. As it was, I was sorely tempted to feed him to the crocodiles in the Jumna River."

THE RAF MEMBERS MEET THE AMERICAN AIRMEN IN KARACHI.

As the planes traveled across India, the searing heat started affecting the Americans. They found it hard to sleep at night and hard to stay cool during the day, and they flew higher than normal to reach more comfortable temperatures. Some RAF pilots at one of their stops took pity on them and gave each one an RAF pith helmet, shorts, and lightweight shirts. The Americans were not used to wearing shorts and ended up with sunburned knees.

Arnold later recalled: "It seems as though there wasn't a breath of fresh air. Perspiration poured off of us. In no time at all we were as wet as though we had fallen overboard. While fixing the planes securely for the night we could literally squeeze moisture from our clothes."

AN AMERICAN-MADE PITH HELMET, SIMILAR TO THE BRITISH ONES WORN BY THE WORLD FLIERS.

While crossing the desert in Sind Province (in present-day Pakistan), the fliers suddenly found themselves in the middle of a large sandstorm. The fine sand stung their faces, got into their clothes, and made visibility difficult. They had to carefully follow railroad tracks, and at first they could not find their next stop, Multan. After several passes over the area, they finally spotted the British troops who were awaiting their arrival. After they landed, the British commander handed each flier a cold glass of lemonade to welcome him to one of the hottest places in India. Arnold commented that the city should be named "Molten" because of its extreme temperature and added, "It certainly is the hottest place that any of us ever hope to visit in this world or the next!"

The following day the fliers continued across the desert, heading for Karachi. Suddenly, the engine of the *New Orleans* started banging and making horrible sounds. Soon oil was spewing out, along with puffs of white smoke. Nelson desperately looked for a place to land in the desert below. Metal pieces from the engine's cylinder started flying off—one ripped a hole in the wing, and another hit Harding's head! The other planes helped by locating potential landing spots and taking the lead to the planned destination. The plane limped along to Karachi, just barely making it. Nelson and Harding were very shaken.

In Karachi, William Douglass, the American consul, greeted the fliers and Wells at the RAF flying base there and handed Smith a telegram. It was from General Patrick

SMITH (*LEFT*) AND WADE SPEAK WITH THE BRITISH
HIGH COMMISSIONER IN BAGHDAD.

in Washington, denying their request to transport Wells. Nothing further was said about the passenger, but Wells's ride was over. The men changed the engines on each plane with help from British mechanics based at the large flying field and repair depot. Arnold made a special note in his journal that they sat down to dinner one evening with ladies, the first time they had done so since leaving the United States.

The airmen continued, without Wells as their passenger, flying over "the most lonesome, barren and desolate place imaginable," with only date trees and cactus, until they finally reached the small port of Bandar Abbas, Persia (present-day Iran). With excellent support from the RAF facilities throughout the British-controlled region, they made good time and were soon closing in on Baghdad (in the recently established kingdom of Iraq). They passed near Basra, the traditional site of the biblical Garden of Eden, and continued on to the former lands of the Sumerians, Chaldeans, Assyrians, Medes, Persians, and caliphs . . . one of the most ancient of all the regions over which they would fly. But they were exhausted from the rigors of flying and from the heat. Only Ogden took time to explore Baghdad during their stop. The rest collapsed into bed, with tender, sunburned knees.

There was a thrill in the mere thought of arriving at Baghdad. And as we descended from the sky and taxied across the largest British aerodrome in the world, which seems to extend to the horizon, we wondered what the ancient story tellers with their tales of the magic flying carpet would have thought if they could have watched us land," said Smith.

They continued their travels through the land of camels. Arnold commented that camels roamed around the same as cows do at home, and he described caravans "silhouetted against the sky exactly as the [movies] sometimes show them." They flew toward Constantinople (present-day Istanbul, Turkey), the sprawling city that straddles the continents of Asia and Europe. The snowcapped Taurus Mountains rose up on the horizon. The Turkish government had been nervous about foreigners flying over Turkish lands and had delayed the U.S. State Department's request for landing privileges, but it finally relented.

After flying through a narrow valley where their wings came uncomfortably close to the cliff walls, the crews looked down on "a sight of cathedrals, minarets, red roofed houses, ancient forts and walls, the ancient city of Constantinople." A few Turkish officials and the American ambassador met them. The fliers had planned to stay just one night, but the Turkish officials requested that members of their military be allowed to inspect

CAMEL CARAVANS AT ONE OF THE REFUELING STOPS. A WORLD CRUISER IS BARELY VISIBLE ON THE RIGHT.

ON THE GROUND, PROBABLY IN BAGHDAD.

LOWELL AND ARNOLD, WITH TURKISH OFFICIALS IN CONSTANTINOPLE.

the planes, so Smith delayed departure by a day, thinking it would be good for diplomacy. The men took a short sightseeing tour and hoped to see the tomb of Alexander the Great, but it was closed. By 7:45 A.M. on July 12, they were back in the air, leaving Asia behind and heading toward the heart of Europe. They had spent almost two months in Asia.

Within four hours they were in Bucharest, the capital of Romania. For once, no official greeting party met them—because they were ahead of schedule! They were happy to service the planes without a crowd of spectators on hand. Arnold liked what he saw of the city: "Bucharest is a clean and snappy looking place, has numerous cafés and cabarets and many well-dressed and attractive looking girls."

The following day they spent a grueling nine hours in the air. They crossed the Carpathian Mountains and followed the mighty Danube River to Vienna, the capital of Austria, with a stop for lunch in Budapest, the capital of Hungary. In Vienna, they were surprised to find a large crowd of mostly American tourists and students welcoming them. They serviced the planes and then drove to the luxurious Imperial Hotel, where their rooms had high ceilings and chandeliers. They were told that the hotel had once been the palace of the prince of Württemberg and that he had lost it in a game of cards. This was a far cry from the tight quarters on a Navy destroyer!

The next morning they were served bowls of raspberries and cream. Arnold enjoyed them so much that he wrote that "it was almost worth flying around the world to eat them."

Although they wanted to stay and soak in more of this grand city, they were eager to reach Paris on July 14, Bastille Day, a national holiday in France. Smith had promised the fliers a leisure day in the French capital if they could arrive a day ahead of schedule. They followed the winding Danube River for several hours, in fog and low visibility. "The rain and fog drove us down to the river and often we shot around sharp bends and kicked rudder just in time to avoid crashing unannounced into a castle." They looked down on trenches, fortifications, and shell holes—the land scarred by the battles of World War I only a few years earlier. In these very skies where they now flew, a new type of warfare—combat between airplanes—had first taken place. After a quick refueling stop in Strasbourg, France, they headed for Paris. What kind of welcome would greet them?

SERVICING THE ENGINES IN STRASBOURG.

A GRAND WELCOME IN PARIS

JULY 14, 1924

A hundred miles from Paris, the Americans were met by an escort of French Aviation Service planes, which led them on a flight over many of the city's famous landmarks, including the Arc de Triomphe, site of the national Tomb of the Unknown Soldier. A crowd of 5,000 was waiting to welcome them. The fliers had enjoyed relative peace during the previous thousand miles or so, but that would now all change. Europe was following their story and eager to see these American celebrities. The crowd waved flags and shouted, *"Vive la France! Vive l'Amérique!"* Wade later said, "During that hour on the outskirts of Paris we met more generals, ambassadors, cabinet ministers, and celebrities than we had encountered in all the rest of our lives. There were so many of them that we couldn't remember their names, despite the fact that they were all men whose names are constantly in newspaper headlines."

The unending routine of early morning departures and long flights had taken its toll on the fliers; they were exhausted. Nevertheless, they accepted their hosts'

invitation to attend a famous Paris cabaret. They were ushered to special seats. But when the lights dimmed for the show, they promptly fell asleep! That night the fliers put signs on the doors to their rooms: "Please do not wake us until nine o'clock tomorrow morning unless this hotel is on fire and not even then, unless the firemen have given up all hope."

The following day was full of "pinch me" moments as both French and American officials welcomed them. They placed a wreath at the Tomb of the Unknown Soldier; then, to their surprise, they sat down to lunch with General John J. Pershing, the famous commander of the American Expeditionary Forces in World War I. Municipal officials welcomed them, and they signed the Golden Book of the City of Paris before heading to the Elysées Palace to meet the new president of France, Gaston Doumergue. He invited them to accompany him to the Olympic Games, in progress nearby. They stood with him

1 AERIAL VIEW OF THE ARC DE TRIOMPHE IN PARIS.

2 OGDEN WAVES THE FRENCH FLAG ON ARRIVAL IN PARIS.

3 CROWDS GREET THE WORLD CRUISERS AT THE PARIS AIRPORT.

SMITH POSES WITH FRECH GENERAL NIESSEL.

to review 4,000 Olympic athletes marching past, and they cheered for the Americans. Doumergue wanted to award them with the prestigious French Legion of Honor medal, but they told him that as military men they were not permitted to accept it without the approval of the U.S. Congress. (They were later given congressional approval and received the medal after their trip.)

After two nights in Paris, they headed back to their planes. At the airport they were impressed by the many commercial flights taking off and landing. Passenger travel in the United States was not yet common. As the World Cruisers took off toward London, they were surrounded by an escort of French fighter planes. The Americans were amazed by the kindness that the French people had shown them and never expected such attention from top military officers. They were, after all, mere lieutenants and sergeants. If the French people were this enthusiastic, what kind of reception would the British people give them?

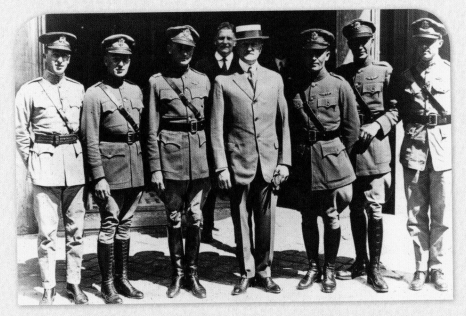

THE WORLD FLIERS MEET GENERAL PERSHING (*CENTER*) IN PARIS.

MEETING ROYALTY IN GREAT BRITAIN

JULY 16, 1924

The relatively short 215-mile flight between the capital cities of France and Great Britain took more than three hours because of stiff headwinds. But finally the planes' wheels touched down at Croydon, south of London, where crowds of reporters, photographers, and autograph hunters were waiting. The British police had to join hands and make a ring around the fliers to escort them to lunch. Mrs. Stuart MacLaren, the wife of the leader of the British around-the-world flight, stepped out of the crowd to thank the Americans for their assistance. The British flight was continuing, heading for the Soviet Union, even as the Americans drew ever closer to their own finish line. Meanwhile, the Italian and Argentine flights were set to begin in a few days.

That night the Americans were guests of the top officials of the British Air Ministry. Wade was so tired that as he sat at the dinner table with a knife and a fork in his hands, a general on one side of him and a lord on the other, he fell asleep and started snoring. As a tickled Nelson wrote later, "Folks insisted on entertaining us, so listening to Leigh's imitation trombone solo was the price we paid."

CROWDS GREETING THE AMERICAN
AIRMEN AT CROYDON, ENGLAND.

The next morning, after a quick flight over the sights of London, the fliers headed to Brough in northern England, the base of the Blackburn Company, a manufacturer of air- and seaplanes. They would undertake major repairs there, replace the engines, and change the wheels to pontoons, making use of the well-equipped facilities. In the last seventeen days they had covered nearly 6,500 miles and made up a lot of time. The airmen were now only two weeks behind their original schedule. However, they faced one of the most dangerous legs of their trip: the North Atlantic Ocean.

The American airmen spent almost two weeks in England. They ventured to London once but otherwise stayed in the vicinity of Brough, happy to have the machine shop and lots of space to work on the planes. Their accommodations were at the airfield, and they appreciated that they didn't have constant observers and interruptions. They were surprised by the number of people asking for their autographs. Arnold wrote that "autograph hunting seems to be a rage here in England."

The fliers had a scare one day as they hoisted the *Chicago* up using a crane and a heavy chain. They had tested the strength of the chain and were satisfied it could easily hold the weight of the plane. Several of them had been working under the hanging plane and had just crawled out when the chain broke and the plane came

crashing to the ground, damaging the pontoons. "We got a big kick out of seeing those two and a half tons fall where we had been just a few seconds before. Of course, it was nobody's fault," Smith recalled.

Even though they worked ten- to eleven-hour days, they managed to get lots of sleep and eat good food. One night they visited a local pub and followed pub tradition: The walls held racks of long-stemmed clay pipes, and the Americans took pipes that hadn't been used, smoked them, wrote their names on them, and put them back in the rack. They were told that no matter how long it took them to return, their pipes would be waiting for them. Another night the airmen visited the country estate of Robert Blackburn, head of the airplane factory where they were doing their work. They glimpsed the life of an English gentleman and were greatly impressed with country living.

One night they were invited to be guests of honor at a banquet sponsored by the Royal Aero Club at the posh Savoy Hotel in London. A whole array of British aristocracy attended: dukes, earls, and other lords and ladies in their finery, as well as Frank Kellogg, the American ambassador. Each flier was announced individually and greeted with applause. Once again they heard many speeches in their honor and received thanks for their role in helping the British flight. The Prince of Wales (who

ARNOLD AND NELSON (*FAR RIGHT*) WITH THE BLACKBURNS,
THE FLIERS' HOSTS AT BROUGH, ENGLAND.

later became King Edward VIII) was upstairs and sent for them, anxious to hear about their trip. They chatted with him for a few minutes, and he bet each of them five dollars that he would beat them to New York—he was sailing in a few days. The fliers returned to Brough, happy to be away from the London limelight.

Days later they received an invitation from the king and queen to attend a garden party at Buckingham Palace. They respectfully turned it down, citing a need to continue work on the planes.

The fliers impressed the British aviation world. A British aeronautical expert who witnessed both the arrival of the planes in Croydon and their departure from Brough wrote to the *New York Times*:

The impressions formed, both of the men and machines, have been wholly favorable and . . . few people in British aviation have any doubt that nothing but rank bad luck can prevent them winning for America the honor of being first around the world by air . . . Everyone here is impressed by the thoroughness with which the American expedition is organized . . . They [the fliers] frankly admit the flight has been one of the hardest jobs they ever tackled . . . There is a general consensus of opinion here that the Douglas World Cruisers are eminently sound and well-constructed machines, a credit to American design and technical skill, while the reliability of the reconditioned and modified Liberty engines is most impressive . . . Undoubtedly this brief visit of the American airmen has done much to bring the two nations more in touch over the ovation, and cordial wishes have been expressed that the individual airmen should return at some future date.

On July 29, the airmen were given the go-ahead to fly the next day. The planes were in top condition, and the men were well rested and ready to leave the comforts of England. They had purchased heavy flight clothing for the cold weather that lay ahead in the Far North.

They flew 450 miles over Scotland, catching glimpses through the cloud banks of beach resorts, cliffs, beautiful estates, and ancient, crumbling ruins. They landed at the Orkney Islands, on the edge of the North Sea, the first of various island stepping-stones across the Arctic. Stopping at a place called Scapa Flow, a large natural harbor that had been Britain's chief naval base during World War I, the fliers saw dozens of half-submerged German warships that had been sunk at the end of the war. They had fun exploring the sunken vessels and climbed the masts of the battle cruiser *Hindenburg*. Arnold reported that Wade lost a bet that he could make a jump from one gun to another; he fell into the fifty-five-degree water, much to the entertainment of the rest of the group.

THE FLIERS BET WADE (*SECOND FROM RIGHT*) THAT HE CAN'T JUMP FROM ONE GUN TO THE OTHER AT SCAPA FLOW.

FLIERS TALKING WITH REPORTERS IN SCOTLAND AFTER THEIR FIRST ATTEMPT TO REACH ICELAND.

PLANE IN DANGER

AUGUST 1, 1924

In preparing to support the World Flight airmen as they traveled across the North Atlantic, the U.S. Navy came up with a plan of placing small fleets of ships at intervals along the route. The ships would help the fliers navigate by sending black smoke out of their funnels fifty minutes before the planes were due at a particular point, to show their location until the fliers passed by. They would also aid in communication. It was very important that the fliers know the weather forecasts for what was ahead of them, and the naval radio system could help. The crews aboard the ships would communicate by placing large boards out on the deck to indicate the weather forecast at the next destination. "T" meant good weather, "L" meant unfavorable conditions, and "H" dangerous flying conditions. The naval crews would also be responsible for setting up mooring buoys and providing small boats for when the planes landed.

As the first ships steamed into position, the weather reports were not good. On August 1, the three planes managed to take off from the Orkney Islands for Iceland, but they immediately hit a fog bank. The pilots couldn't see one another, and the *New Orleans* got separated. The *Boston* and *Chicago* returned to Scotland to wait out the fog. Silence from the *New Orleans* led to worry that something bad had happened. Finally, one of the Navy ships heard from Nelson— whose plane had indeed made it to Iceland. In the fog, he had

U.S. NAVY DESTROYER *BARRY* AT AN UNIDENTIFIED HARBOR—PROBABLY PICTOU HARBOR, NOVA SCOTIA.

gotten into a "propeller wash"—an unpredictable air current generated by another plane—and gone into a downward spin. He just managed to get control of the plane and avoid hitting the water. The *New Orleans* then continued toward Iceland, occasionally encountering fog. The engine ran rough and the oil pressure dropped unexpectedly, and Nelson and Harding wondered if they would ever see land. Eventually, the small village of Horna Fjord, Iceland, appeared before them, and they landed safely.

When the fog lifted, the *Boston* and *Chicago* took off to join the *New Orleans*. Wade later explained what happened next to the *Boston*: "All of a sudden I noticed the oil pressure going down. In a few seconds it dropped all the way to zero. So there was nothing to do but land at once and take no chances on the motor freezing and our falling into a spin." Their altitude was 500 feet, so it was relatively easy to glide to the water. As the plane landed, it left an oil trail in

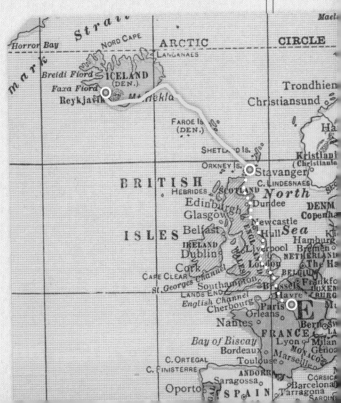

the water, revealing that the engine's oil pump had failed. "When we reached the water I discovered how deceiving the sea is when you are above it. From 500 feet it had looked fairly smooth. But when we landed we found it so rough that the left pontoon wrapped itself completely around the lower wing and snapped two of the vertical wires." Wade signaled frantically that the *Chicago* shouldn't try to land but instead should alert the nearest Navy ship. Smith understood and headed for the destroyer *Billingsley*, almost one hundred miles away.

When it reached the *Billingsley*, the *Chicago* flew over twice, attempting to drop notes onto its deck, but they missed both times. However, a sailor recovered the second note, which was tied to a life preserver. The captain then signaled with three blasts of the ship's whistle that the destroyer was on its way to rescue the *Boston*. Satisfied that their friends were in the capable hands of the Navy, the *Chicago* continued on to Iceland, where the fliers joined the *New Orleans* crew and stayed overnight in a fisherman's hut.

As they watched the *Chicago* fly away, Wade and Ogden on the *Boston* felt very lonely. They were in the middle of the ocean with no living things in sight, not even a porpoise. Wade later said, "Our oil pump could hardly have picked out a more remote spot in which to let us down." Since they had no replacement pump, they would need to be towed or hauled on board a ship. "We hadn't been bobbing up and down on the waves for many minutes before we discovered what a nasty business it is to be in midocean on a fragile plane with the waves hitting her at right angles. Soon we both grew dizzy," said Wade.

THE *BOSTON*, READY FOR A TOW; A PILOT SITS ON THE TOP OF THE LOWER RIGHT WING.

"The waves looked mountain high as they rolled toward us. Only the superb workmanship and the strength of the materials which Donald Douglas had put into these cruisers prevented the *Boston* from being knocked to pieces within an hour."

The men were concerned that the damaged plane—and especially the pontoons—wouldn't be able to withstand the pounding by the waves until help arrived. If not, the plane would sink and the men would die of hypothermia in a matter of minutes. Making matters worse, two of the vertical wires attached to the wings had snapped. Crawling out onto the wings, hanging on for dear life, Wade and Ogden managed to fix the wires. Then it began to rain, and they grew more uneasy. A few hours into their ordeal, they spotted smoke from a ship on the horizon. Wade crawled up on a wing and waved a sheet while Ogden shot off a flare. But the ship did not see them.

At last, four and a half hours after the forced landing, another ship appeared. This time it spotted them! A British fishing trawler chugged toward them: safety in view at last. The trawler attempted to tow the damaged plane but could not do it safely because of the high waves. The men would have to wait for a destroyer. Both the *Billingsley* and the *Richmond* finally appeared and pulled up alongside the plane. The fliers drained the fluids from the plane and emptied it of all loose equipment and

baggage. They attempted to patch a few holes in the pontoons and considered taking off the wings and hoisting the fuselage up to the ship's deck. But then the wind increased, and it wasn't safe for them to remain on the pitching plane.

Wade and Ogden managed to position a sling around the plane and began to hoist it up onto the *Richmond*, using the ship's crane. Suddenly, a large wave hit, and then the five-ton boom crashed down on top of the plane,

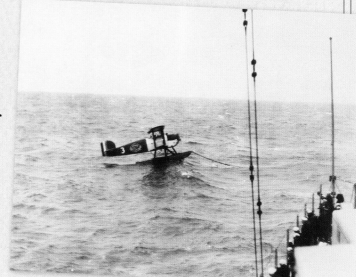

THE *RICHMOND* TOWS THE DISABLED *BOSTON* IN THE NORTH ATLANTIC.

breaking the propeller and punching several holes in the left pontoon and left wing. The storm's intensity increased, and now only two options remained: Continue towing the aircraft or sink it. The damage to the plane was bad, and the storm's intensity was making towing dangerous.

LAST SIGHT OF THE *BOSTON* AS IT SINKS BENEATH THE WAVES.

The ship's captain informed the fliers that the ship itself could be wrecked on the rocks if the plane wasn't cut loose. Finally, Wade uttered the words he dreaded: Abandon the airplane.

The sailors used axes to chop holes in the pontoons and then cut the tow lines. The two fliers saluted their faithful plane and watched as the *Boston* slowly sank into the Atlantic Ocean. With heavy hearts they radioed the bad news to the other fliers, waiting for them in Iceland. It appeared that their participation in the journey was over.

They were, Arnold wrote, "all torn between two emotions, one of relief that Wade and Ogden were safe, and the other of sorrow that after coming 20,000 miles they should so suddenly lose their plane through absolutely no fault of theirs." It was yet another moment of realization that their fortunes could change abruptly, and their flight could be over in a moment. They had safely flown through all kinds of weather and endured other harsh conditions and frightening moments, but one malfunctioning mechanical part had brought one plane's journey to an end. Despite the best planning and full support from the U.S. military, the fliers had now lost two planes—but thankfully, no lives.

Would they make it home?

ICEBERGS AND FOG

AUGUST 5, 1924

The two remaining crews were entering the home stretch now, pressing on in the *New Orleans* and *Chicago* toward Reykjavik, the capital of Iceland. They followed the coast, noting the lack of safe landing harbors available if they encountered mechanical trouble. The airmen saw the hulks of ships that had been wrecked on rocks over the years. They suddenly found themselves in a rare dust storm; the engine of the *New Orleans* began to run rough, and the oil pressure dropped. Rather than attempt a landing in this remote area, they decided to push on.

Gazing at the landscape below, Arnold counted more than forty glaciers and saw many seals on the rocks. He noted,

VIEW OF THE BAY THAT IS FULL OF FLOATING ICE, AT ANGMAGSSALIK, GREENLAND.

"This country plainly shows its volcanic origin and while we failed to see them, there are many smoking craters."

When they reached Reykjavik, the airmen were surprised to find a crowd of 25,000 people cheering their arrival! They landed with no problems, and then the destroyer *Richmond* arrived with Wade and Ogden aboard and gave a greeting whistle. Soon the six fliers were reunited. Wade, tears in his eyes, walked to Smith and gave him a bear hug.

A plan was under way to allow Wade and Ogden to rejoin the flight. In Washington, D.C., General Patrick directed that the prototype World Cruiser on which the other planes were based should be readied for use and painted with the World Flight insignia and the number 3. It would be transported to one of the stops in Maine or Canada, and the two downed fliers would rejoin the journey.

Meanwhile, the two remaining planes had to try to make it through more harsh weather. Reports indicated that the harbor at their next planned stop—Angmagssalik, Greenland—was iced in, which was not unusual for August in the area, and so they had to wait to take off. Various parties went out exploring other possibilities, but no safe harbors could be identified. It was the end of the warm season, and there was worry that all the harbors would soon ice up for the winter. As one newspaper explained, "The ice pack reported to have formed around the Greenland Coast is not considered in itself an impassable barrier to the continuance of the flight, Army experts said, because it had been proved entirely feasible for the planes to land beside vessels at sea and refuel. While the ice itself is not a barrier, should a forced landing be necessary, to [*sic*] rescue of the flyers would be difficult."

As the fliers waited, they enjoyed Icelandic hospitality. The presence of five American warships meant 2,500 sailors there too, as well

THE DANISH MERCHANT STEAMER *HANS EGENDE* IN PACK ICE, PROBABLY SOMEWHERE NEAR FREDERIKSDAL, GREENLAND.

as some newspaper reporters. It was the first time the U.S. Navy had visited the capital. Reykjavik had all the amenities of a modern city, and many of its residents spoke English.

The Icelandic people were enthralled by the World Flight. Arnold later wrote that when the fliers pulled the *New Orleans* out of the water for repair, "Great crowds gathered around . . . all day just looking and looking—this no doubt being the greatest event in Iceland since its discovery."

The fliers' patience was tested once again as the weather kept them in place. Smith heard a rumor that they were going to abandon the flight. Concerned that this false report would reach his superiors in Washington, he sent

THE *NEW ORLEANS* IS TAKEN OUT OF THE WATER FOR REPAIR AT REYKJAVIK, ICELAND.

word to them saying that if the harbor at their next stop didn't open soon, they would fly south to an emergency base at Frederiksdal (present-day Narsarmijit), Greenland. He assured them there were two other options, though both were more dangerous: They could refuel at sea or switch to wheels and fly directly to Labrador (today part of Canada)—a long haul over the ocean. There was no doubt in the fliers' minds that the trip was getting trickier, and that this leg might be the most dangerous yet.

And the race was still in progress, with two new countries tackling the challenge. Argentina had finally joined the competition on July 22. Major Pedro Zanni and his mechanic began their attempt in the Netherlands, taking off from Amsterdam, heading east. The Italian world flier, Lieutenant Antonio Locatelli, and his crew had set out from Pisa on July 25 and were traveling west. The American and Italian flights actually crossed paths in Iceland. The American fliers were eager to inspect Locatelli's plane and were quite impressed: "It appeared to be the most efficient plane for long-distance flying that we had ever seen," said Smith. Locatelli asked the Americans if he could fly with them across the Atlantic, and after some discussion, they decided it was a good idea and received

OFFICERS OF THE *RICHMOND* WITH THE ITALIAN FLIER
ANTONIO LOCATELLI (*SECOND FROM LEFT*).

permission from the Army. They dined with the Italian crew and learned that Locatelli was a member of the Italian Parliament.

Finally, after thirteen days of waiting for the harbor at Angmagssalik to thaw, they decided to fly directly to the emergency base at Frederiksdal instead. This would add 335 miles of ocean and ice fields to an already dangerous trip and would require additional fuel, creating more of a challenge to lift the planes into the air. The official go-ahead came, and the planes lined up to take off. But suddenly a large wave crashed over the *New Orleans* and broke its propeller. Another wave caught the *Chicago* and slightly damaged the front spreader bar. So it was back to shore to repair the damage. Then they received a report that Angmagssalik was unfrozen! However, they had already decided to fly directly to Frederiksdal and did not change their plans. They managed to repair the planes quickly after the parts arrived on the *Richmond*.

Three days after their previous attempt, they finally took off for Greenland, with Locatelli along for the ride. However, he quickly realized that his plane could go much faster and rather than continue to circle the Americans' planes, he abandoned the idea of their flying together. He wagged his wings in farewell and sped away.

As they headed toward Greenland, the Americans spotted the various Navy ships in place along the route, exactly where they were supposed to be. They flew low over the *Billingsley* to wave to the sailors and saw "GOOD LUCK" painted in large white letters on the deck. Next they came upon the *Barry*, carrying Wade and Ogden to Nova Scotia. The ship's flags signaled dangerous weather ahead: fog, rain, and wind.

The pilots were forced to fly close to the water on account of the fog but now feared smashing into an iceberg. Arnold wrote, "It was an unusual sight to us to see a great sea of heaving ice in large and small cakes, ice bergs of all sizes and descriptions floating about and great cakes of ice 'blue' in color standing out sharply in contrast to the white field." Smith wrote later, "We were traveling along at a speed of ninety miles an hour, and could see only between a hundred and a hundred and fifty feet ahead . . . Three times we came so suddenly upon huge icebergs that there was no time left to do any deciding. We simply jerked the wheel back for a quick climb, and were lucky enough to zoom over the top of it into the still denser fog above." They couldn't fly above the fog because of their heavy load, and they knew that the coastal mountains were nearby—and remembered the fate of Martin and Harvey in Alaska.

When the planes encountered a very large iceberg, they had to bank steeply: one plane to the left, one to the right. In the fog they became separated, but finally both made it to Fredericksdal, arriving fifty minutes apart. They had been awake for forty-two hours, eleven of them in the air. Arnold claimed that the weather they had flown through was worse than what they'd encountered in Alaska. Captain Lyman Cotton on the *Richmond* described it as "the longest and most difficult leg of the transatlantic flight . . . a flight to test the skill and courage of the hardiest aviator."

In Fredericksdal, there was no word of the Italian flight. People feared the worst, and a huge search began over a 12,000-square-mile area filled with icebergs. Miraculously, after days of searching and just when the *Richmond* was ready to turn around and go back for more fuel, there was a flicker of light in the distance. They went to investigate and found the Italian plane, with pilot and crew safe. They had landed on the water to wait for

FLOATING ICEBERGS COULD TOWER MANY STORIES HIGH AND CAUSE HAVOC FOR BOTH SHIPS AND THE SMALL PLANES.

the fog to lift, but then the plane had been severely damaged by the ocean and icebergs. It would not have lasted another night. Sadly, the plane could not be salvaged and was sunk.

The American fliers' next jump, to Ivigtut, was only 165 miles, as opposed to the 830 they had flown on the previous leg. This time, besides weather, they could blame the icebergs for a delay. Although they had employed a motorboat to guard their planes and push away any icebergs that moved too close, ice had somehow managed to puncture a pontoon on the *Chicago*. The fliers pumped water from the pontoon, and Smith jumped into the icy sea to patch the hole. Since a man could last only a short time in the freezing water, they took turns and were all soon numb—but the holes were repaired.

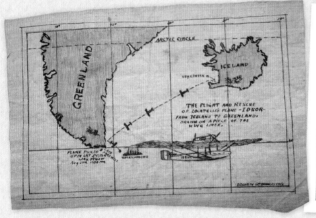

A SKETCH OF THE RESCUE OF THE ITALIAN AIRMAN LOCATELLI BY AN AMERICAN SAILOR, ELECTRICIAN'S MATE SECOND CLASS G. T. BROMLEY, ON A PIECE OF FABRIC TAKEN FROM LOCATELLI'S PLANE BEFORE IT WAS SUNK.

THE AMERICAN AIRMEN WERE CONCERNED THAT A LARGE ICEBERG MIGHT FLOAT INTO THE WORLD CRUISERS AND DAMAGE THEM.

The flight to Ivigtut went well despite more challenging weather. When they arrived beneath overcast skies, the crews pulled the planes up out of the water onto the beach and inspected and replaced engines, as well as replaced and revarnished the pontoons. Despite swarms of tiny biting gnats that drove them crazy and required them to wear netting around their faces and necks, they completed work on the planes in only three days. However, the Navy had not yet moved its ships into place for the next leg of the trip. Thus, their stay in Ivigtut ended up lasting a week. The sun finally came out, and the fliers were able to see the beauty of Greenland. Arnold wrote, "It is very picturesque in a wild rugged way—towering mountains of bare rock covered here and there by patches of green moss which is thick and soft and to walk on reminds one of a deep velvet carpet. Most of these peaks are covered with snow and glaciers and from these, many small streams go rushing and tumbling down the mountain sides. These streams are full of trout and afford a great sport to those so interested—a catch of 30 or 40 being not at all unusual for a two hour trip."

Since it was Arnold's birthday, the fliers went to Ivigtut, where the townspeople, mostly Danish mining families, entertained them. Ivigtut was known for its cryolite mine (a rare mineral used mainly in processing aluminum). The American ship *Island Falk* was anchored there, and the fliers visited it too. Arnold wrote, "To see American movies on an American cruiser in Greenland with the northern lights flashing brightly through the skies is quite a novelty."

On August 31, the airmen were finally given the go-ahead to fly the final leg across the Atlantic Ocean to North America: a 560-mile flight to Icy Tickle, Labrador. It took the *Chicago* two hours of taxiing to get into the air, but the *New Orleans* used the *Chicago*'s wake and was able to take off easily. After early fog the fliers finally hit sunshine, and things looked good—until "the cold hand of Failure suddenly tried to claw us down," as Smith recalled later. The *Chicago*'s fuel pump suddenly failed, and oil began leaking out of the engine. Smith switched to the reserve fuel tank and yelled to Arnold to use the hand-operated wobble pump in his cockpit to keep the engine running. They estimated there was only enough fuel in the reserve tank to fly for two hours or so, but the real question was whether Arnold could keep pumping. After three hours of doing so, his arms were numb and he desperately needed a rest. But the *Chicago* was continuing to lose oil, and the compass wasn't working. Using the sun's position, they aimed west, hoping to see land and a friendly Navy ship.

THE *CHICAGO* IN FLIGHT, LESLIE ARNOLD STANDING IN THE REAR COCKPIT.

13 THE WELCOMING CROWDS OF NORTH AMERICA

AUGUST 31, 1924

hortly after 3:00 P.M. Smith and Arnold spotted the *Richmond*. The ship greeted them with a long blast of its whistle. Welcome to Labrador! Arnold recorded in his journal that the press and movie people were waiting for them. President Calvin Coolidge sent a message: "Your history-making flight has been followed with absorbing interest by your countrymen and your return to North American soil is an inspiration to the whole Nation. You will be welcomed back to the United States with an eagerness and enthusiasm that I am sure will compensate for the hardship you have undergone. Your countrymen are proud of you. My congratulations and heartiest good wishes go to you at this hour of your landing."

THE *CHICAGO* AND THE *NEW ORLEANS* IN INDIAN HARBOR, LABRADOR, AUGUST 31. THE *RICHMOND* WAITS IN THE DISTANCE (*UPPER RIGHT*).

The telegram (U.S. Naval Message) reads in part:

U. S. NAVAL MESSAGE
OFFICIAL BUSINESS

From Chief Naval Operations
To U. S. S. MILWAUKEE
Date 16 August 1924

8816 Following message from the President to be delivered to each member of Army Flight immediately upon arrival at first landing point on American Continent quote Lieut. Lowell H. Smith Flight Commander United States Army comma Lieut. Eric Nelson comma Lieut. Leigh Wade comma Lieut. Leslie P. Arnold comma Lieut. John Harding comma Lieut. Henry H. Ogden period Your return to North American soil following circumnavigation of the earth by air comma is an inspiration to the whole nation period Your history-making flight has been followed with absorbing interest by the people everywhere and you will be welcomed back to the United States with an eagerness and enthusiasm that I am sure will compensate for the hardship you have undergone period Your countrymen are proud of you period Your branch of the service realizes the honor you have won for it period My congratulations and heartiest good wishes go to

① THE TELEGRAM FROM PRESIDENT COOLIDGE WELCOMING THE FLIERS BACK TO NORTH AMERICA.

② THE CREW FROM THE *LAWRENCE* MARKS THE SPOT IN ICY TICKLE, LABRADOR, WHERE THE WORLD FLIERS FIRST TOUCHED THE SOIL OF THE WESTERN HEMISPHERE.

By this point the airmen were anxious to complete the flight, and they all expressed concern about continual delays because of ceremonies, speeches, and parties at each stop along the way. In addition, they were exhausted; they just wanted to get home. They contacted General Patrick and requested that he change the schedule to allow them to fly directly to Seattle. Absolutely not, he replied, and he ordered them to continue on their planned route and to graciously accept the congratulations of their admirers.

Over the next few days, as the *Chicago* and *New Orleans* headed down the Newfoundland coast, the crews saw trees for the first time since Britain, and they passed small fishing villages where it looked as if the entire population—including dogs—was on the beach cheering for them. When they landed at Pictou Harbor in Nova Scotia, they were thrilled to see Wade and Ogden—and their replacement plane, the *Boston II*. Crowds cheered, and every kind of whistle seemed to be tooting. The town honored them with a parade of a Scottish band, American and Canadian sailors, and students. The townspeople had decorated the streets with flags, bunting, signs, and lights. The evening festivities included speeches, a private dinner of lobster and beer, and then a dance.

After a day of bad weather, the three planes—the *Chicago*, the *New Orleans*, and the *Boston II*—were cleared to take off on September 5 for Boston. However, their old foe, fog, forced an unplanned stopover in Mere Point, Maine. They refueled and stayed overnight in cabins that local residents offered them. Local Boy Scouts stood watch over the planes.

The following day at noon, they took to the air for Boston. An escort of ten planes—with the fliers' boss, General Patrick, at the controls of one—joined them. In two short hours they were above Boston, and the extent of their achievement began to sink in.

A huge crowd was waiting to welcome them. Arnold wrote later that "every boat and whistle for miles around was saluting us and guns were fired." The governor of Massachusetts and the mayor of Boston greeted them with a motorcade and a police escort to the state capitol. The streets were lined with cheering throngs, and there were lots of troops and military bands. The fliers were given rooms at a posh hotel and a private dinner by General Patrick, and they even gave a short hello on the radio. They also met the British flight leader, Stuart MacLaren, who was passing through Boston heading home. His flight had come to an end with a crash landing in the Soviet Union's Komandorski Islands.

The American airmen had become celebrities. But they all knew that their flight wasn't officially over. They still needed to reach Seattle to truly achieve their

1 BRASS KEY TO THE CITY OF BOSTON PRESENTED TO SMITH.

2 A BAND GREETS THE AIRMEN AT THE AIRPORT IN BOSTON.

3 THE U.S. ARMY HOSTS A DINNER FOR THE FLIERS IN BOSTON.

goal. Nevertheless, their Army commander made it clear that they must graciously accept the people's admiration: "Our countrymen are very proud of you . . . and they will be eager to show you their appreciation for what you have done." After a day in Boston, where they exchanged the planes' pontoons for wheels, they took off for New York.

Many towns and cities along the route had requested to see the fliers. The airmen flew over Providence, Rhode Island; over Arnold's hometown, New London, Connecticut, where a festival was going on in their honor; and over Manhattan, where they could see thousands of people waving at them from below. They made a single pass over the Statue of Liberty before making a smooth landing at nearby Mitchel Field. A huge crowd broke through security and surrounded them. When the crowd was finally under control, the Prince of Wales appeared and suggested that they settle the bet they had made with him in London. They had lost! His ship had beaten them to New York.

Senator James W. Wadsworth of New York made a speech that was particularly eloquent: "If our hospitality seems ferocious, forgive us because it comes from the heart. You will find as you proceed along the home stretch that these receptions are the first evidence of what all Americans long to show you. The world never forgets its pathfinders. Those who trod the wilderness and cross the seas filled with dangers are never forgotten by posterity."

WORLD CRUISERS FLYING IN FORMATION OVER NEW YORK CITY.

They took to the air again the next day, bound for Washington, D.C., with notice that President Coolidge would be greeting them. They passed over Philadelphia and then Baltimore. But south of Baltimore the engine of the *New Orleans* suddenly stopped. Nelson managed to land in a large pasture. At General Patrick's request, Nelson hopped aboard one of the escort planes, leaving Harding behind to discover that the timing gears had slipped. But the forced landing, combined with strong headwinds and an unplanned fuel stop, meant they were behind schedule. After a three-hour delay they wondered whether the president would still be waiting.

JOURNEY'S END

The planes touched down at Bolling Field outside Washington, D.C.—and sure enough, there were President and Mrs. Calvin Coolidge, as well as most of the cabinet. They had been waiting three hours in the rain. The president had followed the flight's progress around the globe and was eager to meet the airmen. They posed for photographs, and Smith proudly showed the president the *Chicago*.

The stop in Washington included an official visit to the White House; a trip to the office of General Pershing, whom they

1 PRESIDENT COOLIDGE, LOWELL SMITH, AND SECRETARY OF WAR JOHN W. WEEKS STANDING IN FRONT OF THE *CHICAGO* AT BOLLING FIELD, WASHINGTON, D.C.

2 PRESIDENT CALVIN COOLIDGE CONGRATULATES SMITH IN WASHINGTON, D.C.

had met in Paris; visits to injured Army personnel at Walter Reed General Hospital; interviews with many reporters; and a flight over Arlington National Cemetery, where they dropped flowers from their planes near the Tomb of the Unknown Soldier. They stayed in the city for National Defense Day celebrations and were guests of honor in a grand parade down Pennsylvania Avenue. Arnold wrote, "The reception and applause given to us all along the line of march was wonderful—and to be so received by our own people thrilled us all. It was probably the greatest moment in our lives." They then joined the president and First Lady to review the parade.

SMITH, WADE, AND NELSON RIDE IN THE NATIONAL DEFENSE DAY PARADE IN WASHINGTON, D.C.

After a few days in Washington, the World Cruisers took off for Dayton, Ohio, the birthplace of the airplane. They landed at McCook Field, an Army Air Service aircraft center where three of the fliers had been stationed before the journey. They were welcomed by a huge crowd, which included Frederick Martin, their original captain, and his mechanic, Alva Harvey. Here they took a break and allowed the excellent Air Service mechanics to inspect and work on the planes. It was the first time they had allowed this to happen out of their presence. They also underwent a physical examination by the Army to assess their health.

Two days later the three planes took to the air again, getting ever closer to the end of the flight. As they continued, they fell into a routine of adulation: at each stop, crowds awaited, dignitaries welcomed

CARTOON FROM THE *SEATTLE POST-INTELLIGENCER*, SEPTEMBER 17, 1924.

ALL LINED UP FOR THE FINISH LINE IN SEATTLE.

them and gave them official gifts, and local people provided receptions and dances and special accommodations. In Chicago, they attended a large banquet, where they received engraved cigarette boxes filled with gold coins. In Omaha, Nebraska, the citizens had chosen a queen and five ladies-in-waiting to escort them to various events. At a banquet in the small town of Muskogee, Oklahoma, they were given gold medallions. Large crowds gave them a Texas welcome in Dallas and El Paso, and more cheers awaited them in Tucson, Arizona, and San Diego, California.

In San Diego, twenty-five escorts met the fliers in the air. For the first time all three World Cruisers lined up in flight and landed simultaneously. Smith's and Harding's parents were among those who welcomed them. The fliers were taken to a reception in a large stadium filled with 35,000 people. There were more gifts, speeches, and rooms in a fancy hotel. Once again they allowed Army mechanics to install new engines in their planes in their absence. Next, in Santa Monica, a crowd of 200,000 people surrounded them. Smith later described how "the crowd went wild. With a roar they knocked down the fence. They knocked down the police, they knocked down the soldiers. They knocked us down . . . People were tearing bits off our clothes and snipping off buttons for souvenirs. One lady cut a chunk of my collar with a penknife. And another got hold of my ear—I suppose by mistake. Somebody else took a keepsake out of the seat of my trousers." Poor Wade ended up with three cracked ribs as a result of the crowd's enthusiasm.

① THE SIX FLIERS
IN FRONT OF A WORLD
CRUISER.

② THE RELIEVED
FLIERS ARE HAPPY TO
BE AT JOURNEY'S END.

③ THE FLIERS WERE
FEATURED ON THE
COVERS OF MAGAZINES,
SUCH AS SLIPSTREAM.

Finally, they headed for the finish line. First was San Francisco; then Eugene, Oregon; and at last they spotted snowcapped Mount Rainier, just outside Seattle. They again formed into a straight line and landed in unison, to a twenty-one-gun salute. *They had done it!* They had traveled 26,345 miles around the world. Newspaper headlines all over the globe announced the accomplishment. One London paper wrote, "The glory of being first will remain with the Americans."

The fliers were relieved that the trip was over. When a reporter asked Smith if he would do it again, his quick answer was "not for a million dollars . . . unless I was ordered to," and Arnold said, "the best part of the trip—the finish, to have it all over with, to be through with the worry and the strain of it all."

Now they wanted to relax and catch up on sleep. They thought the country would forget about them. But they were wrong. People wrote songs about them and named babies for them; they continued to receive lavish gifts and awards; they even met Orville Wright, one of the brothers who had invented the airplane. While other fliers would eventually break their time record, no one else could ever claim the title:

FIRST FLIGHT AROUND THE WORLD

EPILOGUE

A memorial statue to the first around-the-world flight stands at the entrance of Seattle's Warren G. Magnuson Park, near where the journey started and ended. The wreckage of the *Seattle* was retrieved and is part of the collection of the Alaska Aviation Heritage Museum in Anchorage. Although the *Boston* was never recovered from the North Sea, Maggie— Leigh Wade's stuffed toy monkey and the *Boston*'s mascot— was saved and is on display at the National Air and Space Museum. Neither the *New Orleans* nor the *Chicago* ever flew again. The *New Orleans* belongs to the Natural History Museum of Los Angeles County but is on loan to the Museum of Flying in Santa Monica, California, located near the site of the old Douglas plant where the planes were built. The *Chicago* stands proudly on display at the Smithsonian's National Air and Space Museum in Washington, D.C., part of the Barron Hilton Pioneers of Flight Gallery.

① THE *CHICAGO*, ON DISPLAY IN THE BARRON HILTON PIONEERS OF FLIGHT GALLERY AT THE SMITHSONIAN NATIONAL AIR AND SPACE MUSEUM, WASHINGTON, D.C.

② THE FUSELAGE OF THE *CHICAGO* BEING CARRIED INTO THE AIRCRAFT EXHIBIT BUILDING OF THE SMITHSONIAN INSTITUTION AT WASHINGTON, D.C., IN THE MID-1920S.

RECORDS

★ FIRST TO CIRCUMNAVIGATE THE GLOBE

★ FIRST TO CROSS THE PACIFIC OCEAN

★ FIRST TO CROSS THE CHINA SEA

★ FIRST TO CROSS BOTH THE PACIFIC AND THE ATLANTIC OCEANS

QUICK FACTS

★ TIME IN THE AIR OF THE *CHICAGO*: 363 HOURS, 7 MINUTES (15 DAYS, 3 HOURS, 7 MINUTES)

★ TRIP LENGTH: 150 DAYS

★ TRIP DISTANCE: 26,345 MILES

★ 72 STOPS FOR FUEL AND MAINTENANCE

★ 28 NATIONS VISITED

COMBINED, THE PLANES USED:

★ 15 ENGINES

★ 14 SETS OF PONTOONS

★ 42 SETS OF WHEELS

★ 27,000 GALLONS OF GAS

★ 2,900 GALLONS OF OIL

WHAT HAPPENED TO THE OTHER WORLD FLIERS?

BRITISH FLIGHT	FRENCH FLIGHT	PORTUGUESE FLIGHT	ARGENTINE FLIGHT	ITALIAN FLIGHT
CREW OF THREE	CREW OF TWO	CREW OF THREE	CREW OF TWO	CREW OF FOUR
MARCH 24– AUGUST 4	APRIL 24– MAY 20	APRIL 7– JUNE 24	JULY 22– SEPTEMBER 11	JULY 25– AUGUST 24
CRASHED IN THE SOVIET UNION	CRASHED IN CHINA	CRASHED IN CHINA	PLANE DAMAGED ON TAKEOFF IN JAPAN	PLANE DESTROYED IN THE NORTH SEA

NO LIVES WERE LOST ON ANY OF THESE FLIGHTS.

GLOSSARY

AVIATION: the design, production, and operation of aircraft

BIPLANE: an airplane with two sets of wings, usually one above the other

CARD COMPASS: a small compass attached to a card, not always the most accurate kind

CRANKCASE: the part of an internal combustion engine that encloses and protects the crankshaft

DOUGLAS TORPEDO BOMBER: a plane built for the U.S. military by the Douglas Aircraft Company (1921)

GASOLINE STRAINER: a device for keeping dirt out of an engine

IGNITION LEADS: spark plug wires

MONSOON: very heavy rainfall, usually associated with parts of Asia

PONTOONS: hollow attachments used on seaplanes instead of wheels to help the plane float

PREVAILING WINDS: winds in a certain area that typically blow in a predictable direction

RADAR: a device that uses radio waves to determine the location and speed of an object

SPREADER BAR: a horizontal bar separating the pontoons

TYPHOON: a tropical hurricane in the western Pacific Ocean and China Sea

VOLTAGE REGULATOR: a device that controls the flow of electrical current in an engine

WOBBLE PUMP: a hand pump used to get fuel to an airplane engine when the automatic pump fails

WORLD WAR I: a major war fought mainly in Europe and the Middle East (1914–18)

ITINERARY

Based on the official report submitted by
First Lieutenant Lowell Smith of the World Flight

DATE	LANDING POINT	MILES FLOWN	DATE	LANDING POINT	MILES FLOWN
APRIL 6	Seattle to Prince Rupert, B.C. (CANADA)	650	10	Haiphong, FRENCH INDOCHINA (NOW IN VIETNAM)	495
10	Sitka, ALASKA	282	11, 15	Tourane, FRENCH INDOCHINA (NOW IN VIETNAM)	410
13	Seward, ALASKA	625	16	Saigon, FRENCH INDOCHINA (NOW IN VIETNAM)	540
15	Chignik, ALASKA	425			
19	Dutch Harbor, ALASKA	390	18	Kampongson Bay, FRENCH INDOCHINA (NOW IN CAMBODIA)	295
MAY 3	Nazan, Atka Island, ALASKA	365		Bangkok, SIAM (NOW THAILAND)	290
9	Chichagof, Attu Island, ALASKA	555			
15/16	Komandorski Islands, RUSSIA (DATE CHANGE AT 180TH MERIDIAN)	350	20	Tavoy, BURMA	200
				Rangoon, BURMA	295
17	Paramushiru, JAPAN	585	25	Akyab (now Sittwe), BURMA	480
19	Hitokappu Bay, Yetorofu, JAPAN	595	26	Chittagong, BURMA (NOW IN BANGLADESH)	180
22	Minato, JAPAN	485			
	Kasumigaura, JAPAN	350		Calcutta, INDIA*	265
JUNE 1	Kushimoto, JAPAN	305	JULY 1	Allahabad, INDIA	450
2	Kagoshima, JAPAN	360	2	Ambala, INDIA	480
4–5	Shanghai, CHINA	550	3	Multan, INDIA	360
7	Tchinkoen Bay, CHINA	350	4	Karachi, INDIA (NOW IN PAKISTAN)	455
	Amoy, CHINA	250	7	Chahbar, PERSIA (NOW IRAN)	410
8	Hong Kong, CHINA	310		Bandar Abbas, PERSIA (NOW IRAN)	365

DATE	LANDING POINT	MILES FLOWN
8	Bushire, PERSIA (NOW IRAN)	390
	Baghdad, IRAQ	530
9	Aleppo, SYRIA	450
10	Constantinople (now Istanbul), TURKEY	560
12	Bucharest, ROMANIA	350
13	Budapest, HUNGARY	465
	Vienna, AUSTRIA	113
14	Strasbourg, FRANCE	500
	Paris, FRANCE	250
16	London, ENGLAND	215
17	Brough, ENGLAND*	165
30	Kirkwall, Orkney Islands, SCOTLAND	450
AUG. 2	Horna Fjord, ICELAND	555
5	Reykjavik, ICELAND	290
21	Frederiksdal, GREENLAND	830
24	Ivigtut, GREENLAND	165
31	Icy Tickle, LABRADOR (NOW CANADA)	560
SEPT. 2	Hawkes Bay, NEWFOUNDLAND (NOW CANADA)	315
3	Pictou Harbor, Nova Scotia, CANADA	430

DATE	LANDING POINT	MILES FLOWN
5	Mere Point, MAINE	460
6	Boston, MASSACHUSETTS*	100
8	Mitchel Field, NEW YORK	220
9	Aberdeen, MARYLAND	160
	Washington, D.C.	70
13	Dayton, OHIO	400
15	Chicago, ILLINOIS	245
17	Omaha, NEBRASKA	430
18	St. Joseph, MISSOURI	110
	Muskogee, OKLAHOMA	270
19	Dallas, TEXAS	245
20	Sweetwater, TEXAS	210
	El Paso, TEXAS	390
21	Tucson, ARIZONA	280
22	San Diego, CALIFORNIA	390
23	Los Angeles, CALIFORNIA	115
25	San Francisco, CALIFORNIA	365
27	Eugene, Oregon	420
28	Vancouver Barracks, WASHINGTON	90
	Seattle, WASHINGTON	150

*WHEEL/PONTOON CHANGES

ENDNOTES

Complete bibliographic information for the works cited below appears in the Bibliography.

① THE JOURNEY BEGINS

5   "Gentlemen, you have arrived . . .": Thomas, 51.

5   SIDEBAR "More than 400 years . . .": President Calvin Coolidge, message to the fliers, April 2, 1924; copy in National Air and Space Museum Archives.

② PLANNING THE TRIP

6   "The writer wishes to . . .": Delmar H. Dunton to the chief of the Air Service, November 9, 1923. Copy in National Air and Space Museum Archives.

③ FIERCE WINDS IN ALASKA

16   "woolies—a sudden gust . . .": Arnold journal, April 24 and 25, 1924.

16   "Some of [the] gusts . . .": Arnold journal, April 24 and 25, 1924.

17   "A gale suddenly swept . . .": Thomas, 82–83.

18   "I've heard of 'bad . . .": Arnold journal, April 30, 1924.

14   SIDEBAR "A river of solid . . .": Arnold journal, April 13, 1924.

14   SIDEBAR "the clear deep blue . . .": Glines, 51.

14   SIDEBAR "This evening the moon . . .": Arnold journal, April 14, 1924.

18   SIDEBAR "Rather cold on the . . .": Arnold journal, April 27 and 28, 1924.

④ DISASTER ON THE MOUNTAIN

20   "To expect outside rescue . . .": Glines, 61.

22   "Ship a total wreck . . .": Glines, 63.

22   "While there is nothing . . .": Letter, Major Martin to General Patrick, June 3, 1924, quoted in *New York Times*, June 4, 1924.

22   "The experience gained, the . . .": Harvey, 14–15.

21   SIDEBAR "It was a terrible . . .": *Atlanta Constitution*, May 12, 1924, 1.

⑤ FIRST ACROSS THE PACIFIC

23   "The Aleutians have but . . .": Arnold journal, May 5, 1924.

23   "We have only two . . .": Glines, 67.

24   "everything was one color . . .": Thomas, 63.

24   "like lead shot being . . .": Glines, 48.

25   "It was heartening news . . .": Glines, 68.

25   "given a real treat . . .": Arnold journal, May 14, 1924.

25   "rolling and tossing like . . .": Thomas, 107.

27   "The first flight in . . .": Glines, 72.

27   "We are all greatly . . .": Arnold journal, May 17, 1924.

⑥ COLORFUL JAPAN

28   "nice change to pass . . .": Arnold journal, May 19, 1924.

56 **SIDEBAR** "The impressions formed, both...": The British aeronautical expert C. G. Colebrook, quoted in *New York Times*, August 3, 1924.

⑪ PLANE IN DANGER

59 "All of a sudden...": Lowell Thomas, "Thrilling Adventures of the World Fliers," *Washington Post*, January 20, 1925, 20. All quotations about this incident are from this source.

62 "all torn between two...": Arnold journal, August 4, 1924.

⑫ ICEBERGS AND FOG

64 "This country plainly shows...": Arnold journal, August 5, 1924.

64 "The ice pack reported...": *Los Angeles Times*, August 7, 1924, 1.

65 "Great crowds gathered around...": Arnold journal, August 9, 1924.

65 "It appeared to be...": Thomas, 270.

66 "It was an unusual...": Arnold journal, August 21, 1924.

67 "We were traveling along...": Thomas, 273.

67 "the longest and most...": Thomas, 272.

68 "It is very picturesque...": Arnold journal, August 28, 1924.

69 "To see American movies...": Arnold journal, August 29, 1924.

69 "the cold hand of...": Thomas, 288.

⑬ THE WELCOMING CROWDS OF NORTH AMERICA

70 "Your history-making flight...": President Calvin Coolidge, message to the fliers, August 16, 1924; copy in National Air and Space Museum Archives.

72 "every boat and whistle...": Arnold journal, September 6, 1924.

73 "Our countrymen are very...": Glines, 147.

73 "If our hospitality seems...": *Aviation*, September 22, 1924.

⑭ JOURNEY'S END

75 "The reception and applause...": Arnold journal, September 12, 1924.

76 "the crowd went wild...": Thomas, 312.

77 "The glory of being...": Editorial, *Times* (London), September 30, 1924.

77 "not for a million...": Glines, 159.

77 "the best part of...": Arnold journal, September 28, 1924.

BIBLIOGRAPHY

BOOKS

Glines, Carroll V. *Around the World in 175 Days: The First Round-the-World Flight*. Washington, D.C.: Smithsonian Institution Press, 2001.

Glines, Carroll V., and Stan Cohen. *The First Flight Around the World, April 6–September 28, 1924: A Pictorial History*. Missoula, Mont.: Pictorial Histories, 2000.

Harvey, Alva. *Memoirs of an Around-the-World Mechanic (1924) and Pilot (1941)*. Manhattan, Kans.: Air Force Historical Foundation, 1978.

McKay, Ernest A. *A World to Conquer: The Epic Story of the First Around-the-World Flight*. New York: Arco, 1981.

Thomas, Lowell. *The First World Flight: Being the Personal Narratives of Lowell Smith, Erik Nelson, Leigh Wade, Leslie Arnold, Henry Ogden, John Harding*. Boston: Houghton Mifflin, 1925.

Wells, Linton. *Blood on the Moon: The Autobiography of Linton Wells*. Boston: Houghton Mifflin, 1937.

NEWSPAPERS AND MAGAZINES

Atlanta Constitution

Aviation

Boston Daily Globe

Chicago Daily Tribune

Los Angeles Times

New York Times

Times (London)

Washington Post

DOCUMENTS

Leslie Arnold Journal: United States Army Around the World Trip (Leslie Arnold) Collection, Archives Department, National Air and Space Museum, Smithsonian Institution, Washington, D.C.

Other documents: United States Army Around the World Flight (1924) Collection, Archives Department, National Air and Space Museum, Smithsonian Institution, Washington, D.C.

ACKNOWLEDGMENTS

Many people supported my effort to write this book. I'd like to thank my National Air and Space Museum colleagues Trish Graboske, Maureen Kerr, Diane Kidd, Jeremy Kinney, and Beth Wilson for their careful review of the manuscript. Jeremy is keeper of the *Chicago* (lucky guy) and was always willing to answer strange questions. Melissa Keiser and the other staff in the National Air and Space Museum Archives provided excellent guidance in searching the large World Cruiser collections. I valued Melissa's sharp eye and suggestions for photographs. Thanks, too, to Benny Glassman, age ten, for his thoughtful comments about the manuscript. Lastly, a thank-you to editor Howard Reeves for taking a chance on this unknown story and for lending his vision to the project. My hope is that this grand adventure story, now brought into the light again, will inspire new generations.

ART CREDITS

INDEX